Rejection

JOHN WHITE

Rejection

Addison-Wesley Publishing Company

READING, MASSACHUSETTS • MENLO PARK, CALIFORNIA
LONDON • AMSTERDAM • DON MILLS, ONTARIO • SYDNEY

ISBN 0-201-08310-8 (pb.)

ISBN 0-201-08311-6 (counterpack)

ABCDEFGHIJ–HA–898765432

"Enough of the sweet smell of success. It's time to study the fetid fragrance of failure." —GERARD O'CONNOR, *teacher-philosopher*

The greatest rejection of them all

Acknowledgments

For this book, profoundest thanks go to Gardner Cox, whose rejection engendered it, and to *Harvard Magazine,* which nursed it along with a fine fat story in July-August 1980 and kindly gave permission to use big chunks.

Thanks of a different sort go to Jim Cornell and Jean Martin, placer and shaper; Harvard's Widener, Hilles, and Observatory libraries, nourishers; Joan Wedd, Lydia Foote, Placidia Carter, and the Up Country ladies, keepers of the rain off; Alice Mary Pierce, Marjorie LeMay, Florence McCulloch, Grace Forbes, and Sue Ames, listeners; Nick Basbanes, forbearer; and IBM, special effects.

Doe Coover breathed life into it, and Roberta Biery helped fasten to it that tail by which the eel of knowledge can be held, the index.

Immeasurable thanks go to these generous gatherers and sharers, without whom, almost literally, nothing:

China Altman, Jim Ames, Carolyn Amundson, Roberts Appel, Janet Barnes, Kemp Battle, Wendy Beck, both Benets, Susan Bliss, Joe Brooks' Harriet Taub, Tom Burnam, Hildreth Burnett, Barbara Ninde Byfield, John Camp, Jean Carefoot, Adrienne Carney, Paul and Julia Child, Deborah Clifford, Olivia Constable, Kittymouse Cook, Rosamund De Lap, all Drexels, all Durants, both Earlys, Mickey Fuller, Theodor Gaster, both Haileys, Ibby Halsted, Richard Harland, all Hayeses including Nelson, Susan Hirschman, Linda Hirschmann, Betty

Proxmire

United States Senate
COMMITTEE ON BANKING, HOUSING, AND
URBAN AFFAIRS
WASHINGTON, D.C. 20510

December 2, 1981

John White

Dear John:

Here are some answers to your questions.

Question. What is the most rejectable thing you have ever found unrejected?

Answer. The space shuttle. It is an uneconomic project which will never pay off and which was built at the cost of billions including a massive overrun.

Question. What is the worthiest thing which has been rejected?

Answer. The Renegotiation Board. It examined military contracts let by non-competitive methods to make certain the taxpayer didn't get robbed. In a period of negotiated contracts it is essential but fell to the lobbying of the contractors.

My criteria is whether it is a) a worthy program or project, and b) whether it either costs too much or saves money for the taxpayer.

Foolish research--I prefer the term low priority research for a lot of research which is not necessarily foolish is marginal or unneeded--must cost more than $2 billion a year.

I think the Golden Fleece Awards are great. They started in March of 1975 and have been given monthly since then. In the first year two-thirds of the programs given the award were either stopped or cut back. I have received no thanks from either the government or the recipients. They send brickbats but the taxpayers cheer.

No, I know of no similar award although a lot of people have started to imitate it.

I hope this is helpful.

With best wishes.

Sincerely,

William Proxmire, U.S.S.

WP:hsd

nen, Richard Saunderson, Seymour Slive, Norm Sperling, Bud Stillman, Bob Storey, Umeko, Armar and Greg Strauss, all Szaparys, Bill Terry, both Thompsons, Abigail Trafford, Doug Tsuruoka, Joy Vargas, Virginia Pierce, both Vernons, Frank Waldrop, both Welches, Phil Weld Sr. and Jr., Bob Wetmore, Joan White, Chuck Whitney, Burke Wilkinson, both Willemins, Phillip Wingate, Richard Wolfe, Larry Wylie, Bill Youngman.

"Many hands make light the work."

For *light* read *possible.*

These lighted up dark corners: Elizabeth Cavendish, Mariah Gregory, Priscilla Hallowell, Peggy Huddleston, Lisa King, Rita Monahan, Sandra Peterson, Robert Riggs, Joannie Shurcliff, Lisa and Carmen Tedesco, Ellen Thurman, Robb White. The gnomes of Ferranti-Dege Cameras kept the art faithful.

Drawing by Charles Addams; © 1956 The New Yorker Magazine, Inc.

For inspiration and occasional corroboration, these contributed invaluably if unwittingly: *The Book of Lists* I and II, the *People's Almanac* I and II, *Movie Facts and Feats*, Helen L. Kaufmann's *Story of One Hundred Great Composers*, Stephen Pile's *Incomplete Book of Failures*, *Time*, and *TV Guide*.

Any benefactors whose names are not here will please forgive. They have simply been misfiled or something. Not forgotten. Not r-------.

It is customary for authors, having thanked all of their helpers, to make a pretty statement exonerating those helpers from any blame for any mistakes in the book. *Mea culpa!* They claim, somewhat as terrorist groups claim credit for bombings, responsibility for every possible error.

This author is not going to do that.

There are doubtless scores of mistakes in this book—how could there not be?—such anecdotes travel far in space and time, being manhandled all the way, and they are born unto distortion as the sparks fly upward. Everybody who touches one is liable to bend it.

There is plenty of blame to go around, and the author accepts only his share of it.

Let him who is without slippage cast the first law suit.

However, readers who spot especially egregious errors, of omission as well as commission, are beseeched to send corrections, additions, suggestions, whatnot, to the author in care of this publisher.

Go, little book—and, rejected or accepted, sit tibi bonum.

Introduction

Feeling blue because you didn't get that job, that girl, that approval?

Was your idea not accepted by the boss—you not accepted by the voters, or by any of the seventeen colleges you applied to?

Are people dumping on you?

Life got you by the throat?

Bravo!!

Join the club.

President—Michelangelo; Vice President— Beethoven; Secretary—Whistler's mother. Members—Rodin, Mozart, & Company.

Where you are now, they were.

Like you, they all knew rejection.

Rejection is a much abused word. We tend to think of it as the same thing as failure, but that isn't always so.

Re-jec-tion—the very sound of it is wounding, like a knife cut, presaging humiliation, defeat— the end.

But that's not the way it has to be.

We may *think* of it as only those bad things, but we *act* on it quite differently. Often enough we take it as challenge, illumination, inspiration—the beginning.

In a Thackeray story, "The Rose and the Ring," while the other guests at the christening of Princess Rosalba are wishing her happiness, beauty, success, and so on, good Fairy Blackstick, the wisest of them all, says "the best thing I can wish her is a *little misfortune.*"

Most rejection is rooted in simple good judgement, of course. That which is offered is not good enough. That kind is usually benefi-

A little misfortune

cial, leading to improvement of the product, but not much is heard of it because it is reasonable and undramatic.

As this book will show, rejection can be, like smoking, dangerous to your health, as it was for weapons expert Christopher Cooke, or even, as it was for architect Edgar Chambless, fatal.

But it can also be the best thing that ever happened. That's what it was for Tom Edison, Julia Child, Monet (and Manet), Thoreau, Christ, Rembrandt, Hitler, the boss of Piggly Wiggly, and the state of Texas. And that's what it is for most of us, most of the time.

If it wasn't, we wouldn't be here.

Narrowly defined, *rejection* means only passive avoidance or refusal to accept or active throwing away. But in practice the word can mean anything from negative avoidance or throwing away through neutral ignoring to positive selection (which implies rejection of the unselected).

What it is for you is not so important as what it does to you, and you to it.

All kinds of people, ideas and things have been rejected in all ages, all places, all kinds of ways, for all kinds of reasons, with all kinds of results.

Rejection has many roots.

It can come from cruelty, benevolence, anger, or absurdity.

Aristides of Athens (530–468 B.C.) was such a good ruler (so "great and illustrious," Plutarch said, that he was "the admiration of all Greece") that he was called "Aristides the Just." He was doing his usual excellent job when suddenly the people voted to banish him. During the ballotting an illiterate man, not

Aristides the
Just

recognizing him, asked him to write "Aristides" on his ballot. Aristides asked the man whether Aristides had ever injured him. "No," said the man, "nor do I even know him; but it vexes me to hear him everywhere called 'the Just.' "

Rejection can be insulting, charming, helpful, painful, brave, obnoxious, fearful.

On the night before the Crucifixion Peter denied Christ thrice. (Later, after he had served as the steadfast Rock of the Church for thirty years, he went bravely to his martyr's death.)

Peter denying Christ

It can be selfish. Many people classified as "insane" have merely rejected this sad world for one of their own, or none. Tchaikovsky deliberately drank unboiled water and died of cholera.

It can even be longed for but unattainable. A King of Siam used to give to any courtier whom he wanted to destroy a white elephant that ate a lot and required expensive care and which, like the Godfather's offer, could not be refused.

Rejection comes in many shapes.

Sometimes it is public, as in the case of a national election. Sometimes it is private, a pink slip of dismissal stealthily tucked into one's office mail. (Bosses never say that a worker has been "fired"—they say that he has been "let go," as if he had won permission to quit an oppressive confinement.)

Sometimes it comes like a roaring lion, as it did on that wild night in 1913 when the Paris audience turned into a mob and demolished *The Rite of Spring.*

Sometimes it is silence. "Don't call us—we'll call you." Sometimes it isn't. "Dear John." Sometimes it is shared, as when the postman rings twice; sometimes it isn't, as when there is no postman, only a computer.

Giuseppe di Lampedusa sent the manuscript of the only book he had ever written to a publisher. The letter of rejection was so measured and calm that the old aristocrat saw no reason to disagree with its finding. He hid the manuscript and died thinking that his life's work was worthless. After his death the manuscript was discovered, resubmitted to a publisher, and published. As *The Leopard* it became a bestseller on both sides of the ocean and was made into a movie.

Frankie shot Johnny.

(In general, women take personal rejection harder than men do, because their deepest concerns are people and feelings, especially sympathy and affection. Men tend to be more hurt by professional rejection, because their deepest concerns are thoughts and things, especially the things of work. Let both sides reject that ukase and cry "sexist!"—the women will do so because they feel that they shouldn't feel so strongly, the men because they think that they really do feel more.)

Sometimes it is quirky.

A man sent to Dickens, for publication in his magazine, *Household Words,* a metrical contribution titled "Orient Pearls at Random Strung." Dickens replied, "Too much string."

American poet A. Wilber Stevens got back from his hoped-for publisher a little pile of ashes.

Sometimes it is transcendent.

"And the devil, taking him up into a high mountain, showed unto him all the kingdoms of the world in a moment of time. And the devil said unto him, All this power will I give thee, and the glory. . . . And Jesus answered and said unto him, Get thee behind me, Satan. . . ."

Sometimes it comes as all business, as a presidential veto, and sometimes it comes as all mush—"I'd love to go out with you this evening, but I've got a terrible headache." Sometimes it comes and goes without your even knowing it, as when you are passed over for a promotion.

Sometimes it comes from within, as when your body rejects a transplant. Nature, of course, is full of it.

Some people reject the very principles upon which a society is based.

American singer Paul Robeson rejected his country and settled in Russia; Russian writer Aleksandr Solzhenitsyn was rejected by his country and settled here. England rejected Byron and Oscar Wilde.

Solzhenitsyn
Harvard Theatre Collection

Robeson
Christopher S. Johnson

Wilde

". . . the coward does it with a kiss, the brave man with a sword!"
—Oscar Wilde

W.C. Fields used to keep his extra money in a sock. The great comedian always figured that everybody was a robber but he decided to patronize a different kind of robber, and for the rest of his life he put his extra money into savings banks under fake names like "A. Pismo Clam" or "Egbert Sousé." Then he'd rub his hands and snarl, "Now let the bastards try to find it!"

When he died nobody knew how many hundreds (thousands? millions?) of dollars he had deposited in how many banks in how many countries, under what names.

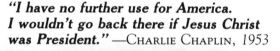

"I have no further use for America. I wouldn't go back there if Jesus Christ was President." —Charlie Chaplin, *1953*

Harvard Theatre Collection

It comes, it comes. . . .

. . . and it bears strange fruit.

Response to rejection varies as widely as human nature.

For author Burke Wilkinson it is "the grain of sand in the oyster—the irritant which causes the oyster to make a pearl."

In 1863 a group of artists got tired of being rejected by the all-powerful Paris *Salon* and set up an exhibition of their own—and started the impressionist movement.

Brigitte Bardot got rid of her puppy fat and spots, and Fred Astaire kept on dancing.

Mary Cassatt hid her picture.

Edward Fitzgerald sent the manuscript of his translation of *The Rubáiyát of Omar Khayyám* to

the editor of *Fraser's Magazine* in 1858; a year later he had heard nothing, so he retrieved it and published it at his own expense—which, it soon appeared, was a very smart thing to do.

In 1978, when ex–Secretary of State Henry Kissinger was still the most famous Man about the World in the world, artist Gardner Cox painted a portrait of him. Kissinger rejected the painting, and there was a three-day tempest in media teapots. Cox was astonished, because, he said, "portraits get rejected all the time, often because in a painting done over a period of days a face can show a mosaic of different emotions, which never happens in photography, or life. The subject may recognize, but not like, what he sees." He put the picture aside—the uproar made it notorious—and within hours he was offered $2000 more for it than the State Department would have paid.

© 1981 Peter Jones

Spain's Salvador Dali proposed to Gala Eluard, was rejected, and said if she didn't change her mind he would jump off a cliff. She did so he didn't have to.

The daredevil motorcyclist Evel Knievel starred in a 1977 movie called *Viva Knievel!* Critics voted it one of The Worst Films Ever Made. He hit one of those critics with a baseball bat and went off to jail.

Rejection has always been with us. It is older than Eve. According to an old Jewish legend, our First Mother was not the first woman. After God had made Adam out of dust He made for him, also out of dust, a wife named Lilith. Lilith got tired of Adam and flew away to the Red Sea. That was all right. But then the Lord made Eve, and she and Adam disobeyed the very first commandment, "of the tree of the

"Watergate Expulsion," by Robert Pryor © 1973 The New
York Times Company. Reprinted by permission.

knowledge of good and evil, thou shalt not
eat," and God rejected the pair of them, and
all of our troubles—and our opportunities—
began.

Rejection will doubtless be with us when our
world ends—probably with a bang of rejection,
and a whimper of a reject.

There are three things to remember about
rejection.

1. It is not the same as failure.

2. It is two-way—all while we are being rejected, personally and professionally, we are rejecting in the same (well, maybe not exactly
the same) ways.

3. Rejection is necessary. Lack of it can be
disastrous. Ross Lockridge and Tom Heggen
both scored spectacular success with their first
books and—very probably partly because of fear
of failure, an unknown quantity—killed themselves before trying another book. Once upon
a time not long ago a young girl who shall be
nameless because her family is still vulnerable—
bright, amiable, adorable, and worthy—got

through the first twenty years of her life without experiencing a rebuff harsher than being told to go back and wash her ears. In college she fell in love with a nice average boy who after six months got tired of her in an average way and moved on. She took forty sleeping pills (being bright, she took them in a secret room where she knew she wouldn't be found for at least three days—one more than it takes for those things to do it.)

What could be more frightening than the spectre of rejection, when you don't know what it is? Only after living with it can you recognize it as a best friend.

Rejection comes in many shapes, some very strange, and by many, and strange, paths—bringing more good than evil.

It need not be and usually isn't the final push over the cliff.

It can be and usually is a momentary, and valuable, setback, a time of learning, sharpening, strengthening.

That is the message of this book.

"We are not amused." —QUEEN VICTORIA

Rick Stafford

More than a dozen publishers rejected a book by the poet e e cummings. So when it was finally published it had this dedication: "No Thanks to: Farrar & Rinehart, Simon & Schuster, Coward-McCann, Limited Editions, Harcourt, Brace, Random House, Equinox Press, Smith & Haas, Viking Press, Knopf, Dutton, Harper's, Scribners, Covici, Friede." (cummings must have been upset to put all of those capitals in.) Finally published . . . by whom? By e e's mother.

Writers, to hear them tell it, get rejected faster than they can write. Over and over and over again.

Roger Tory Peterson's *Field Guide to the Birds*, now a birder's bible, was rejected by five publishers before Houghton Mifflin took it.

What ultimately became one of the favorite children's books of all time, *The Tale of Peter Rabbit*, was prenatally "courteously rejected" by the English publisher Frederick Warne and then "returned with or without thanks by at least six [other] firms," author-illustrator Beatrix Potter noted. (According to an almost certainly apocryphal story one rejecter commented that the tale "smelled like rotting carrots.") Finally she took her savings and paid for publication herself. The little book sold so well that Warne changed his mind, took over publication, and voilà! That was more than eighty

1

years ago, and Peter Rabbit and his friends are still selling briskly.

Peyton Place, that ersatz *Desire Under the Elms,* a mish-mash of small-town sex steamy enough to tempt, you would think, all profit-minded publishers (and what other kind, you might ask, is there?), was turned down by fourteen of them. A work as different from *Peyton Place* as can be imagined, William Appleman Williams's *The Tragedy of American Diplomacy,* was rejected by more than twenty publishers before it was finally accepted. It has now been reprinted several times and is recognized as an outstanding revisionist work. *Jonathan Livingston Seagull* also flew through some twenty rejections.

Irving Stone's first book was about Van Gogh. He took it to Alfred Knopf, and "they never opened it—the package with the manuscript got home before I did." He took it to Doubleday. Everybody liked it except the sales department—they said, "There is no way to sell a book about an unknown Dutch painter." After fifteen more rejections the book, *Lust for Life,* was finally accepted and published in 1934. It has now sold about twenty-five million copies.

As might be expected, James Joyce's writings excited some splendidly grandiose rejections. His *Dubliners* was refused by twenty-two publishers and then shot down in flames by an irate citizen. As Joyce reported it, "When at last it was printed some very kind person bought out the entire edition and had it burnt in Dublin— a new and private *auto-da-fé.*" The odyssey of

Please pardon our short-sightedness and timidity . . .

2

his *Ulysses* was even more spectacular—it was rejected, in fire, by two governments. Parts of the novel were serialized in the New York *Little Review* in 1918–20, and after rejection by a U.S. publisher the whole book was published in France in 1922 by Sylvia Beach's Shakespeare Press. Copies were sent to America and England. They were, reported Joyce, "Seized and burnt by the Custom authorities of New York and Folkestone." Not until 1933 was the U.S. ban on *Ulysses* lifted; the book was published by Random House the following year.

James Joyce
The Poetry/Rare Books Collection University Libraries of the State University of New York Buffalo

Dr. Seuss, the creator of a whole menagerie of lovable floppy monsters, many of which have strayed into radio and TV, survived initial rejection by some two dozen publishers, and according to legend *Gone With The Wind* survived thirty-eight. (Very much "according to legend"— according to Burke Wilkinson [an author of eleven successful books who had his latest, *Zeal of the Convert,* now optioned by Hollywood, rejected fourteen times], "Harold Latham, the conscientious editor at Macmillan, learned about *GWTW* early, commuted to Atlanta to keep Margaret Mitchell tracking, and truly no other firm ever saw the manuscript.")

James M. Cain's novel *The Postman Always Rings Twice* stirred up something of a sensation when it was first published in 1934. It wasn't about the postal service, it was about sex. Cain explained that he had given his book its odd title because before it was accepted for publication it was rejected many times, and each day that the postman brought a letter of rejection he rang twice.

Thank you very much for your contribution. Of course, we depend on such unsolicited contributions and ordinarily . . .

3

REJECTION

Gentlemen, Regarding the recent rejection slip you sent me.

I think there might have been a misunderstanding.

What I really wanted was for you to publish my story, and send me fifty thousand dollars.

Didn't you realize that?

Sometimes it seems—to writers—that the number of possible rejections of a would-be book is limited only by the number of publishers. Says the 1978 *Guinness Book of World Records*, "The greatest number of publishers' rejections for a manuscript is 106 for *World Government Crusade* by Gilbert Young. . . . His public meeting in Bath, England, in support of his parliamentary candidacy as a World Government candidate, however, drew a crowd of one."

Lee Pennington has been published in more than 300 magazines—and rejected so many thousand times that in one six-month period he papered all four walls of a room with rejection slips. ("I loved getting the $8\frac{1}{2} \times 11$ rejections more than the 3×5 ones because they covered more space.") He has also filled scrapbooks with rejection slips, used them for coasters, and given rejection parties—invitations written on the backs of rejection slips.

Other suggested uses for those slips: make lampshades of them, laminate coffee tables with them, make (as does Muriel Rukeyser) wastebaskets of them. Put them on the refrigerator so you won't eat so much.

Believe me, in any other time . . .

4

Pennington once wrote a poem about William Faulkner, sent it off, and got back a two-page single-spaced rejection, the first two sentences of which read, "This is the worst poem in the English language. You are the worst poet in the English language." He burned that rejection letter (an act he has since repented—it would have graced his scrapbook) and sent the poem to another magazine, which accepted it "with glowing praise," and chose it as its year's best poem.

Before William Saroyan (who became one of this country's most published authors) got his first acceptance he had a pile of rejection slips thirty inches high—maybe seven thousand in all.

Actually, we are afraid that it is too good for us . . .

©David Kherdian

william Saroyan
age 57
Fresno, July 21, 1965 for
the Bibliography

Publishers say, somewhat defensively, that their rejections are different from those of other rejectors, not necessarily based on value judgements. They may like a manuscript, they say, but be unable to publish it because of prior commitments or scheduling jams or lack of money or other such operational obstacles. Still and all, they have let some amazingly big fish slip through their nets, ultimate blockbusters of all varieties: *War and Peace, The Good Earth, The Sun Is My Undoing, The Fountainhead, To Kill a Mockingbird, Rubáiyát, Watership Down* . . . . The list goes on and on.

There is a story in the trade that a publisher once accepted a book and sent it to an artist for illustrations. When he had finished the artist sent the manuscript back—and it was returned to him with a rejection slip.

So many books rejected by so many publishers so many times—how do those murdering bastards *feel* when they strangle yet another unborn child? William Styron's 1979 novel, *Sophie's Choice*, tells it like it was in 1947 when the hero was a forty-dollar-a-week reader for McGraw-Hill. The "lusterless drudgery" of trudging through the "club-footed syntax" and "unrelenting mediocrity" of manuscripts like *Tall Grows the Eelgrass*, by Edmonia Biersticker ("fiction . . . may be the worst novel ever penned by woman or beast. Decline with all possible speed."), and *The Plumber's Wench*, by Audrey Smillie (". . . absolutely imperative that this book never be published"), so stupefied the poor wretch that when a manuscript

The idea of Lebanon for dyslexia research just doesn't work . . .

about a "long, solemn, and tedious Pacific voyage" made by "men adrift on a raft" fell into his hands he recommended rejection—"maybe a university press would buy it, but it's definitely not for us"—and the book was *Kon-Tiki*.

You surely didn't expect . . .

Schlesinger Library, Radcliffe College

A reject is a reject is a reject. It is said that Gertrude Stein submitted poems to editors for twenty years before one was accepted.

Books in Print *for 1980–81 lists 521 titles under "Success," 8 under "Failure." Under "Rejection," none.*

So far from being a book for the general reader that nothing can be done about it . . .

Small, cosmetic changes can open doors. Longmans, Green rejected a manuscript titled *The Problems of the Single Woman* only to see it become a bestseller after publication by another house as *Live Alone and Like It.* The same thing happened to a reject called *The Birds and the Bees.* It went on to prosper as *Everything You Always Wanted to Know About Sex* but Were Afraid To Ask.*

"Dear Editor: The volume of rejection slips that I receive makes it impossible for me to answer each one individually."
—Any writer

The poet A. Wilber Stevens, now Dean of the College of Arts and Letters at the University of Nevada at Las Vegas, once sent a manuscript to the editor of a literary magazine whom he knew slightly. When his self-addressed return envelope came back to him he opened it and out fell a little pile of ashes.

Half-cracked . . .

A man supposedly sent a story to the *Reader's Digest* titled, "How I Made Love to a Bear." It was rejected. He rewrote it a little and retitled it "How I Made Love to a Bear in an Iron Lung" and sent it back. Again *Reader's Digest* rejected it. Another rewrite, another title change, to "How I Made Love to a Bear in an Iron Lung for the FBI," and another rejection. This time he didn't bother to rewrite at all—he just lengthened the title to "How I Made Love to a Bear in an Iron Lung for the FBI and Found God." Back came a telegram of acceptance.

We Blacks know all about rejection.

As a wandering storyteller (of that antique tribe of which Jesus was the best) telling stories in streets, in fields, in jails, I deal with rejection much of the time.

Out of the night of rejection come the great stories of light—
>   to the hungry they bring bread,
>   to the naked, bright raiment,
>   to the prisoner, hope.

Brother Blue
Brother Blue, Storyteller

Julia Child & Company/James Scherer for WGBH, Boston

There is a half-baked belief among non-kitchen-minded folk that the culinary bible *Mastering the Art of French Cooking* was a much-wanted child, called into existence to satisfy a demand created by the popular TV series, *The French Chef*. Not so. *Mastering* started life as a twice-rejected orphan.

In 1953 Houghton Mifflin signed a contract with Julia Child, Simone Beck, and Louisette Bertholle for a book with the working title *French Cooking for the American Kitchen*. Five years later the three cook-writers submitted their manuscript, an 850-page compendium called *French Sauces and French Poultry*. Houghton Mifflin rejected it. The next year they brought back a drastically revised 684-page version titled *French Recipes for American Cooks*. Houghton Mifflin rejected that too.

Knopf accepted it and published it in 1961 with the *Mastering* title. Though large and ex-

We feel that perhaps if you make a few changes: Josh a nuclear inspector instead of a retired insurance salesman, Paula the widow of an astronaut, Rod a Social Security claims adjuster . . .

pensive, it sold fairly well right from the start. Impressed by the book's success, public television dreamed up the series *The French Chef,* starring Julia Child, which made its debut on February 11, 1963. That series was a smash hit (pardon the expression) from the cavalier flipping of that first famous potato pancake onto the stove; *Mastering* mastered the air. That same year it was a Book of the Month Club selection, and on November 25, 1966, Julia Child made the cover of *Time* magazine.

If the book (augmented by a second volume in 1970) were a record it would have gone platinum by now—it has sold more than a million copies.

Verily, verily the stone which certain builders rejected is become a head of the corner.

Another head of that corner, Irma Rombauer's inimitable *Joy of Cooking,* is also, apparently, a salvaged reject. According to a memoir written by her daughter, the late Marion Rombauer Beck, a small *Joy* was first privately printed in 1931. "Mother's friends made sales lively, but not brisk enough to suit her," so she added some recipes and tried the marketplace. Only after "making the rounds," meaning, presumably, being rejected by various publishers, was the fattened *Joy* accepted, by Bobbs-Merrill, in 1936. When Irma Rombauer died in 1962 her book had sold six million copies.

In the case of *Mastering the Art of French Cooking,* Knopf seems to have outguessed Houghton Mifflin, but Knopf has not always been so prescient. In 1955 Laurence Wylie, Harvard's esteemed professor of French civili-

Your novel of spying in Washington is timely and well written but we have already published two books on that subject in the last year and . . .

Rick Stafford

zation, sent the manuscript of a sensitive
chronicle of French country life, *A Village in the
Vaucluse*, to Knopf. Back it came with a letter
of rejection which said, "It is so far from being
a book for the general reader that nothing can
be done about it." Wylie did nothing "about"
it—he sent it on to the Harvard University
Press, which published it the next year. It became and has remained an extremely popular
book for the general reader and the scholar
alike. And Houghton Mifflin, as we shall see,
was very prescient in publishing two books that
brought their authors more fame than they
could digest.

> *"Beware of allowing a tactless word, a rebuttal, a rejection to obliterate the whole sky."* —ANAIS NIN

Ross Lockridge's first novel, *Raintree County,* was never rejected. Houghton Mifflin published it in January 1948 and on February 27 Lockridge got word that it had become the country's number one bestseller; on March 6 he asphyxiated himself. Tom Heggen's first novel, *Mister Roberts,* was not rejected. It was published, also by Houghton Mifflin, in 1946, and became a bestseller at once; in 1948 it was turned into the smash hit play. In May 1949 Heggen took an overdose of pills and drowned himself.

In your telegram you say that you sent us a manuscript last September. Can you remember to whom you addressed it?

Query: If those two quick-bloomers had been forced to climb the ladder of success in the usual way, gradually, step by step—been slow-fired in the furnace of rejection—would they be alive today?

In his definitive book about them, *Ross and Tom,* John Leggett doesn't answer that question. How could he? How could anybody separate and measure the impacts of success, failure, challenge, and the responses—hope, fear, joy, motion, emptiness?

> *"Failure is the foundation of success, and the means by which it is achieved. Success is the lurking-place of failure; but who can tell when the turning point will come?"*
> —LAO-TSE

W. Somerset Maugham had surmounted many rejections when he rang the big bell with *Of Human Bondage* in 1915. He weathered that storm of success gracefully enough and went on to other triumphs.

A southern writer named John Kennedy Toole wrote a comic novel about life in New Orleans called *A Confederacy of Dunces*. It was so relentlessly rejected by publishers that he killed himself. That was in 1969. His mother refused to give up on the book. She sent it out and got it back, rejected, over and over again. At last she won the patronage of Walker Percy, who got it accepted by the Louisiana State University Press, and in 1980 it won the Pulitzer Prize for fiction.

After it had won that prize critics fell all over themselves praising it, as if to soothe the dull cold ear of death—but when the dust had settled it seemed that the book wasn't really all that good; the Pulitzer judges were not immune to feelings of displaced guilt.

I remember looking at your novel (cookbook?) with pleasure but I cannot for the life of me remember what I did with it. Could you send another? This time I promise I will hang on to it. (Could I have taken it with me on that Club Med vacation? Have you ever been to the Peloponnese?)

A classic example of authorial rejection-of-rejection, positive response to negative challenge, is Samuel Johnson's celebrated letter to the Earl of Chesterfield. English teachers love to quote that, and it is indeed a masterful display of articulate, muscular rage—even if it might have been uncalled for.

As told by most of those teachers, the story is as simple as it is infuriating. Johnson, overworked and poor in health and in pocket, labored alone for years to put together his monumental *Dictionary of the English Language*, a Herculean task that would have daunted a whole library full of ordinary scholars; many times he appealed to the eminent Lord Chesterfield for patronage that would have been vastly helpful, but his desperate pleas were not answered; then, when the *Dictionary* was completed, about to be published and stirring up favorable comment, the Earl graciously allowed his countenance to shine upon it, and Johnson fired off the famous letter:

The reason for our long delay is that our managing editor died. Hang in there.

Seven years, my Lord, have now past since I waited in your outward rooms, or was repulsed from your door, during which time I have been pushing on my work through difficulties, of which it is useless to complain, and have brought it, at last, to the verge of publication, without one act of assistance, one word of encouragement, or one smile of favour. Such treatment I did not expect, for I never had a Patron before. . . .

Is not a Patron, my Lord, one who looks with unconcern on a man struggling for life in the water, and, when he has reached ground, encumbers him with help? The notice which you have been pleased to take of my labours, had it been early, had been kind; but it has been delayed till I am indifferent, and cannot enjoy it; till I am solitary, and cannot impart it; till I am known and do not want it. I hope it is no very cynical asperity not to confess obligations where no benefit has been received, or to be unwilling that the Publick should consider me as owing that to a Patron, which Providence has enabled me to do for myself.

A well-deserved demoliton of a would-be bandwagoner? Not necessarily so.

In his authoritative biography, *Samuel Johnson*, W. Jackson Bate says that in 1747, when the *Dictionary* was a'borning, a "Plan" of the huge project, dedicated to Chesterfield, was published. The Earl "expressed his interest . . . and sent a gift of £10," enough money in those days to rent a room for two years. Johnson called on his benefactor and found him "exquisitely elegant," with "more knowledge than I expected." (Bate says that Chesterfield was noted for his "good sense," "integrity," and knowledge of languages.) During the next seven years the "aging and weary" Earl was caught up in his work as Secretary of State and had many worries, including crippling arthritis, and forgot about the *Dictionary*. When a friend told him that it was finished he publicly praised it, "more from courtesy and a belated stirring of

I changed jobs and it seems that I forgot to tell my successor about your . . .

conscience than any thought of the honor of being associated with the work"—and was hit by Johnson's letter.

There was a fire in the basement where we store material . . .

"Chesterfield accepted the rebuke with good nature," Bate says, "and was also quite impressed by the letter." He left it on a table where any visitor could see it, "and, reading it aloud to Dodsley, he said, 'This man has great powers,' and 'pointed out the severest passages, and observed how well they were expressed.' "

He also said, according to Bate, that he "would have turned off the best servant he ever had, if he had known that he denied him to a man who would have always been more than welcome."

The reporter of that revealing episode was Robert Dodsley, a publisher noted for the un-Johnsonian gentleness of his own rejections. Sample:

Mr. Dodsley presents his compliments to the gentleman who favoured him with the enclosed poem, which he has returned, as he apprehends the sale of it would probably not enable him to give any consideration. He does not mean by this to insinuate a want of merit in the poem, but rather a want of attention in the public.

The kindly spirit that had animated Mr. Dodsley was still alive in the next century. In 1847 Charlotte Brontë (using the name Currer Bell) sent the manuscript of *The Professor* to a publishing house named Smith, Elder. That firm's letter of rejection actually encouraged the author: it discussed the book's merits and de-

Oblique Mr. Dodsley was an eighteenth-century Londoner, yet he would have been completely at home in the modern, ever inscrutable Orient. There, a writer received this rejection—if so gross a word could be applied to so delicate an instrument—from the publisher of a Chinese economic journal:

We have read your manuscript with boundless delight. If we were to publish your paper it would be impossible for us to publish any work of a lower standard. And as it is unthinkable that, in the next thousand years, we shall see its equal, we are, to our regret, compelled to return your divine composition, and to beg you a thousand times to overlook our short sight and timidity.

merits "so courteously, so considerately, in a spirit so rational, with a discrimination so enlightened, that this very refusal cheered the author better than a vulgarly expressed acceptance would have done." (Later that same year Smith, Elder published *Jane Eyre*.)

Steps Leading Nowhere could be the title of a real-life story written in the blood (if you could call it that) of our literary Solomons not so long ago.

Ezra Pound? " . . . brilliant but an ass."
—WILLIAM CARLOS WILLIAMS

T.S. Eliot said that April is the cruelest month, and he was right. It is the month in which most colleges reject most applicants.

In 1969 *Steps,* a novel by the well-known author Jerzy Kosinski, won the National Book Award. Six years later a freelance writer named Chuck Ross, to test the old theory that a novel by an unknown writer doesn't have a chance, typed the first twenty-one pages of *Steps* and sent them out to four publishers as the work of "Erik Demos." All four rejected the manuscript. Two years after that he typed out the whole book and sent it, again credited to Erik Demos, to more publishers, including the original publisher of the Kosinski book, Random House. Again, all rejected it with unhelpful comments—Random House used a form letter. Altogether, fourteen publishers (and thirteen literary agents) failed to recognize a book that had already been published and had won an important prize.

I have moved to another office, closer to the elevator and with louder neighbors but more storage space, so I truly hope that I will be able to get to your manuscript before too long . . .

Proust

Gide

The Bettmann Archives

In 1911 Marcel Proust had 800 pages of what was ultimately to become the huge complex of novels called *Remembrance of Things Past* ready for publication. Where? Who would accept such an actionless, plotless sprawl of innerness revisited? He approached the house of Fasquelle and was rejected. He went to the *Nouvelle Revue Française* and was rejected again, by a very special rejecter—the celebrated writer André Gide. After a third publisher, Ollendorf, had refused his manuscript (with the comment that it took him thirty pages to tell how he turned over in bed), Proust decided to pay for publication himself.

Eugène Grasset published *Du Côté de chez Swann (Swann's Way)* in November 1913. Gide read it, and the following January wrote to Proust apologizing for the rejection, which he called the "gravest error of the N.R.F. . . . one of the most burning regrets, remorses, of my life." He explained that he had considered Proust a "snob" and a "social butterfly," had only glanced at his manuscript, and has been unimpressed by what he had glimpsed: "My attention fell into the cup of camomile tea . . . then wandered . . . to the phrase [about] a forehead through which vertebrae could be seen." He asked pardon. Proust forgave him and the two became good friends.

One of our readers has been working hard for Handgun Control and two others are getting married this summer so you see why . . .

Proust went on to become more famous than his rejecter, but he was never awarded the Nobel Prize for Literature, as Gide was in 1947.

Emily ("You cannot fold a flood") Dickinson had only seven of her poems published in her lifetime (now her collected words actually fill a fat volume) but her rejecter became her friend. In 1858 Thomas Wentworth Higginson of the *Atlantic Monthly* issued an appeal for fresh talent and the Belle of Amherst sent him some of her poems. He thought her a "half-cracked poetess" and advised her not to try to get anything published. But he did offer friendship and they corresponded for several years.

Our mail room says they have no record of . . .

The Thoreau Society, Inc.

Oddly enough Thoreau's *Walden*, an unprecedented work so offbeat that one would suppose that no publisher would have dreamed of giving it house room, was not rejected. Ticknor and Fields published it at their own risk in 1854, and while by no means a success it was not a total failure: by 1859 the first printing of 2000 copies was sold out. Perhaps this author's well-known defiant attitude helped launch his unusual book without the usual multi-publisher refusal. As he said in *Walden*, "I do not propose to write an ode to dejection, but to brag as lustily as a chanticleer in the morning, standing on his roost, if only to wake my neighbors up."

Have you checked your local post office?

> *". . . there are people for whom [writer's block] . . . may be construed as nature's way of sending you a rejection slip."*
> —R.D. ROSEN, *writer*

Lewis Carroll rejected rather than was rejected, pictures rather than words. He paid for initial publication of *Alice's Adventures in Wonderland* (then titled *Alice's Adventures Under Ground*) by Macmillan in 1865 but he and his illustrator, John Tenniel, were dissatisfied with the quality of the reproductions in the first printing and rejected it. (Subsequent printings pleased author, illustrator, publisher and public.) Carroll got another artist, Henry Holiday, to illustrate *The Hunting of the Snark*, published by Macmillan in 1876, but he rejected one of Holiday's pictures, a very important one. It will be remembered that the *Hunting* ends when the Baker meets the Snark, shrieks, and disappears—because the Snark is a Boojum and as everybody knows it is the fate of whoever meets a Boojum to "softly and suddenly vanish away."

In response to your telegram and telephone calls please accept my apologies for loss of your manuscript which must have . . .

> *". . .of making many books there is no end (so what the hell happened to mine?). . . ."*
> —*Ecclesiastes* 12:12, *modified*

In a way it is a pity that you sent your manuscript to . . .

Holiday drew a picture of the Boojum as a great squat indistinct figure radiating mindless power, oddly reminiscent of phase two of the explosion of an atom bomb, and very frightening indeed, and Carroll rejected it because it was too good. The unimaginable had been imagined, and that shouldn't be.

In 1889 Macmillan published a juvenile version of *Alice* (which psychologists never tire of saying is not really a children's book) with twenty of the Tenniel pictures enlarged and colored, and Carroll rejected the first printing because, he said, the colors were too gaudy. The rejected books were sent to a New York publisher who re-rejected them because, he said, the colors were too dull. (More whimsical Carrolliana may be found in Martin Gardner's books about Alice and the Snark.)

William Saroyan rejected the 1940 Pulitzer Prize for his play *The Time of Your Life* because, he said, business had no business judging art.

Rudyard Kipling composing "The Absent-Minded Beggar"

Rudyard Kipling was rejected three times for his country's highest literary honor. He was a world famous writer when Tennyson's death left the post of Great Britain's Poet Laureate vacant in 1892. Kipling was passed over and the honor was given to a relatively unknown author, Alfred Austin. When Austin died in 1913 Kipling was even more famous—in 1907 he had won the Nobel Prize for literature; again he was rejected for a less eminent writer, Robert Bridges. In 1930 the title was given to John Masefield.

It has been said that one reason for Kipling's rejections was his poem "The Widow at Windsor," which cast Victoria as a Queen whose dominions cost the lives of her soldiers.

I don't realistically think that we will be making any acquisitions this year because the editor-in-chief will be a new father in August . . .

Has it really
been two years?
This office was
reorganized . . .

In any case, the reject's name became familiar to more people than those of all the lofty Laureates together. The most popular picture post card ever devised (six million sold) showed a young couple. He: "Do you like Kipling?" She: "I don't know, you naughty boy, I've never kippled."

(A man once rejected a vendor's offer to sell him some "pornographic post cards" because "I haven't got a pornograph.")

"Sometimes even good old Homer nods."
—Horace

Sometimes even the best of our writers nod. Here, mainly from that lovely book, *The Stuffed Owl* (D. B. Wyndham Lewis and Charles Lee), are some outstandingly bad lines from good writers (bad writers don't matter because they get rejected before they hit print):

Harvard College Library

writers don't matter because they get rejected before they hit print):

"Her smile was silent as the smile on corpses three hours old." —Earl of Lytton

"He fell upon his hands in warm wet slop." —Alfred Austin

"Thou little bounder, rest." —John Ruskin (speaking to his heart)

"A fly that up and down himself doth shove." —William Wordsworth

Wordsworth, poet laureate of England from 1843 to 1850, was especially prone to nodding:

"This piteous news so much it shocked her,/ She quite forgot to send the Doctor."

"The silent heavens have goings-on."

"That is a work of waste and ruin;/ Consider, Charles, what you are doing."

"The Squire is come, and, as I guess,/ His little ruddy daughter Bess."

Kipling said that authors should do their best to reject their own work, on the grounds that no matter how good a piece of writing might seem to the writer it could always be improved by reworking, and especially improved by shortening. (His own corpus could certainly have benefited by extensive rewriting and massive excisions.)

What, any author might add, could be more conducive to rewriting than the goad of rejection?

There was once in Paris a society composed of playwrights who had been hissed. They met once a month on an ill-omened day, Friday, and among their members were the young Dumas, Zola, and Offenbach.

Dumas

Is it true that Hugh Hefner was working for Esquire and asked for a five-dollar raise, was refused, and quit and started Playboy *magazine?*

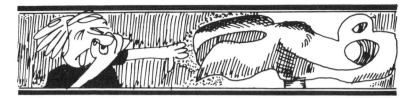

Art works of all kinds are rejected, in all sorts of ways. One of the most ambitious sculptures ever conceived was rejected, unrejected, rejected again, unrejected again, and so on— for thirty-seven years.

In 1505 Pope Julius II commissioned Michelangelo to create for him a vast funeral monument, to be erected in the apse of the new basilica of Saint Peter's Cathedral in the

"Build thee more stately mansions, O my soul, as the swift seasons roll . . ."
—Oliver Wendell Holmes

Julius II

Vatican. Michelangelo designed a structure approximately on the scale of the Sistine Chapel—a rectangular mausoleum, measuring about twenty-three by thirty-six feet at the base, consisting of three tiers tapering into a pyramid, decorated by forty life-sized statues and many sculptured façades and figures. Using marble especially selected in Carrara, he went to work. But there were frustrating delays, and the Pope, possibly influenced by Michelangelo's enemies, ordered the sculptor put out of the Vatican.

Michelangelo

Julius died in 1513, and, as directed by his will, Michelangelo resumed work, with a contract for a second, amended, design. Three years later the structure was still unfinished, and a contract for a third design was made. The work dragged on, and by 1522 the heirs of Julius began asking for the deposit money back;

in 1524 they threatened to go to law; in 1526 Michelangelo proposed a fourth design. The heirs did not accept it. In 1532 Michelangelo signed a contract which bound him to complete a fifth design in three years. That contract expired without the work being finished. In 1542 a sixth contract, which turned out to be the last, was signed. After that the much-amended project, so whittled away by nearly four decades of dilatoriness and bickering and attempted rejection as to be practically unrecognizable, was finally completed.

Today you may see it not in Saint Peter's but in the little church of San Pietro in Vincoli by the Esquiline Hill, a relatively simple façade with inset figures. One of those figures, that of Moses, is the only one of the forty statues originally proposed for the first design that was actually executed and survived to the end. Art historians call the façade a "patched-up solution" and refer to the whole messy business as the "tragedy of the tomb."

San Pietro in Vincoli

If Julius (who doesn't even rest under the patched-up solution—his remains, says a *Guide Bleue*, were "scattered" in 1527) had rejected Michelangelo's proposed monument thoroughly in the first place his memorial would not have become an earthly patch-up—it would have remained an ethereal magnificence on the drawing board.

A half-century ago Cambridge revered her eminent, autocratic, theatrical scholars, and the last class of Denman Ross was an important occasion. Professor Ross, world authority on Oriental art, was renowned for his courtly, kindly, mien, his imperturbable gravity, and his Olympian pronouncements, delivered in what has been described as a "fat, flat, brown velvet voice." The hall was filled for the solemn valedictory. After the lecture there was a surprise ceremony: a student came to the dais and presented the professor a vase that he had found in China. The vase was supposedly ancient, a rare treasure, and there was anticipatory silence as the great man turned it in his hands and looked at it carefully. Then he said to the student, in that brown velvet voice, "You take it."

In 1891 the *Société des Gens de Lettres* commissioned Rodin to carve a monument to Balzac. The sculptor was fascinated by the author, in whom he recognized a kindred spirit—the vast scope of Balzac's cynical *Human Comedy* novels was matched by the breadth and coloration of Rodin's planned *Gates of Hell*. For seven years Rodin immersed himself in Balzac's works, scrutinized contemporary portraits, and visited his native Touraine. Using models who looked like Balzac he made about fifty studies. Then he produced his master work, an extraordinary statue of a man wrapped carelessly in a formless robe (Balzac often wrote in a dressing gown), his head thrown back arrogantly, his rough-cut face contorted with passions almost too powerful, it seems, for bronze to confine—love, hate, perception, compassion, contempt—all are there, and more. That face, bursting with emotion, is pure driven energy—the pilgrim is at the gate of hell.

Auguste Rodin, *Monument to Balzac.* (1897–98) Bronze (cast 1954), 8′10″ high, at base 48¼× 41″, Collection, The Museum of Modern Art, New York. Presented in memory of Curt Valentin by his friends.

The nineteenth-century sculptural mold, showing calm men in period costume making pontifical gestures, was broken to bits.

Rodin's *Balzac* was exhibited at the Salon of 1898 and plunged the art world into wild turmoil. Critical opinion was divided between unrestrained admiration and shocked detestation ("snow man," "toad in a sack"). Within three months nearly a hundred articles either fiercely attacking it or equally fiercely defending it had appeared. For a time that statue was a *cause célèbre*, the center of a controversy as furious as that which was then swirling about *L'Affaire Dreyfus*.

And it was rejected.

Admirers offered to buy the statue but Rodin refused, and kept it in his garden at Meudon for the rest of his life.

The effect of the controversy was to heighten the sculptor's reputation, and in 1939, twenty-two years after his death, the first bronze cast of the statue was erected in the streets of Paris. Rodin's *Balzac* is now one of the recognized glories of France.

A postscript: Rodin was rejected three times for admission to the École des Beaux-Arts in Paris

---

Balzac rejected some things himself. He distrusted photography, fearing that the camera would somehow tear away one of the spiritual layers that encased the body. Considering that in those days a subject had to be strapped into a device like a straitjacket—one subject said

that it was like the famous instrument of tor-
ture, the Iron Maiden—and stay in it without
moving for many minutes while the camera
drank in his essence, Balzac's fear was somewhat understandable.

Frederick MacMonnies, *Bacchante (and Infant Faun)*, American (1863–1937), bronze, 30.521, bequest of Mrs. Harriet J. Bradbury, Museum of Fine Arts, Boston.

While Rodin was working on his *Balzac* another sculptor, Frederick MacMonnies, was
creating a statue as delicate as Rodin's was massive, a nude nymph holding a bunch of grapes
above a laughing baby cradled in her left arm.
Charles McKim, architect of the just-com-
pleted Boston Public Library, liked Mac-
Monnies's *Bacchante and Child* so much that he
offered it to the library as a gift, to be placed
on a fountain in the interior courtyard as a
memorial to his wife. In July 1896 a small study
of the statue was submitted for inspection to a
panel of eminent connoisseurs selected by the
Boston Art Commission to judge the propriety
of the city's library accepting—and displaying—
such an unclothed figure. It was the opinion of
some that the "idealizing of a woman dancing
in a drinking revelry was inappropriate for a library," but permission was granted to allow the
statue to be put in place. On November 11 *The
Boston Post* ran a story headlined *Bacchante
Coming. Art Commission Will Set Up Naked
Drunken Woman for Inspection.* On November 15,
a Sunday, there was a private viewing. That

"Uppity women get stomped on."
—David McLelland, *Harvard professor of
psychology*

night a minister, the Reverend James Brady, preached a sermon against "strumpetry," the pure Boston air was filled with outraged cries, the *Bacchante* was removed, and she never again saw library light. In May 1897 McKim withdrew his offer. Now the pretty girl stands demurely in the Metropolitan Museum in New York and there are replicas in Boston's Museum of Fine Arts and in Paris, but the library's fountain is as bare as was its intended occupant. *Sic transit gloria—pudor vincit omnia.* Rejection can have twisted roots.

Contrary to popular legend, however, that kind of *pudor,* or shame, did not conquer a lightly clad image of the father of his country. According to a notorious story as evergreen, and nevertrue, as the one about the cherry tree, an Italian sculptor long ago carved an immense statue of George Washington wearing only a sort of skirt—the statue was shipped to the new Capital City (although in one version of the story it never reached its destination because it fell through the bottom of the boat) and promptly became a source of such embarrassment that it was hidden away in some basement where it still lurks, its lamentable immodesty mercifully covered with dust. Not so. The truth is that Boston-born sculptor Horatio Greenough was commissioned to carve a statue of the first President in 1832, the centennial of his birth. Greenough was then working in Italy and he carved a large, symbolic, godlike figure, a classic hero surrendering the Roman broadsword of war and assuming the toga of lawgiver. The fifteen-ton statue arrived in Washington in 1841 and was installed in the Capitol Rotunda,

National Museum of American History

but it was feared that it might be too heavy for the floor and in 1843 it was moved to the Capitol grounds. In 1908 it was given to the Smithsonian Institution and set up in the west wing of the old Tower Building. In 1963 it was moved to its present position of honor on the second floor of the Museum of History and Technology.

In 1876 Augustus Saint-Gaudens submitted a "plaster sketch" of a small recumbent female figure dandling an infant to the National Academy of Design exhibit. It was rejected. He was so angry that he helped to found the American Art Association (later known as the Society of American Artists).

The great Praxiteles once carved two Aphrodites, one clothed, the other not, for the people of the island of Cos. Cos rejected the unclothed one; neighbor Cnidus was happy to take the reject because she would attract more sailors.

Claes Oldenberg's giant sculptured *Lipstick*, made of steel, aluminum, and fiberglass, stands (on tank treads) twenty-two feet high and weighs almost two tons and offended a lot of people when it was unveiled in 1969 at Yale University in New Haven, Connecticut. They made earnest efforts to reject it, but failed. It now seems to be a permanent feature of Yale's skyline.

In 1975 the Renault Company rejected a massive sculpture that Jean Dubuffet was working on outside the automaker's plant near Paris. The sculptor sued to be allowed to finish the piece, lost the suit, and appealed. Then Renault carried the rejection to the end of the line—and below. Saying that it needed to "protect" the sculpture during the legal process, it buried the *oeuvre* in the ground. Renault paid Dubuffet his commission of $85,000 for an uninterrupted view of some dirt.

"God pity the artist, for his critics never will." —ANONYMOUS

Claes Oldenburg, *Lipstick Ascending on Caterpillar Tracks*, Yale University Art Gallery, gift of the Colossal Keepsake Corporation.

Pictures of all kinds get rejected as well. A century ago progressive French painters were at the mercy of the all-powerful Salon, which provided one of Paris's very few exhibition galleries and practically dictated which pictures the government and the museums should buy. Like most entrenched ruling bodies, it was rigidly conservative and quick to deny exhibition space to nontraditionalists. In 1863 the Salon selection jury for the annual art show was especially arbitrary, rejecting more than four thousand paintings with the curious pronouncement that the flood of artists should be dammed. The "dammed" painters protested so violently that Emperor Napoleon III ordered a special exhibition of the rejects. That exhibition, the notorious *Salon des Refusés* ("Show of Rejected Artists"), was a sensation. Displaying like a field of bright flowers the lovely new visions of Monet, Manet, Degas, Pissarro, Sisley, Renoir, Cassatt, and their friends, it marked the birth of impressionism.

Van Gogh was too young to be among the 1863 *Refusés*, but later he earned that title many times over. In his whole life he sold only one painting (*The Red Vine*, for 400 francs, in 1890).

Fogg Art Museum, Harvard University, Bequest-Collection of Maurice Wertheim, Vincent Van Gogh, *Self-Portrait* (1888), 1951.65

Daumier kicks
painting

And portraits get rejected all the time. Lyndon Johnson rejected one painted by Andrew Wyeth's brother-in-law, Peter Hurd. (He said it was the ugliest thing he had ever seen.) Winston Churchill tried his best to reject one painted by Graham Sutherland, but he couldn't because it had been paid for by Parliament. (He said, it is told, that it made him look like a toad. After it was safely out of sight in his house, his wife Clemmie broke it and had it burned.) J. P. Morgan rejected a picture of himself taken by the photographer Edward Steichen.

It is an old fable among the unknowing that John Singer Sargent didn't quite make it to the top rank of artists because he never had to challenge himself, his portraits being so facile that they were never rejected. Fact is, his now-famous *Portrait of Madame Gautreau* was resoundingly rejected even before it was finished ("skin too purple"), and Sargent became one of America's greatest portrait painters.

Fogg Art Museum, Harvard University, Grenville L. Winthrop Bequest, John Singer Sargent, *Portrait of Madame X (Mme Gautreau)*, 1943.316

When Hogarth dedicated his *March to Finchley* to George III, that monarch asked a courtier, "Pray, who is this Hogarth?" "A painter, my liege," the man replied. "I hate painting," declared the King, "and poetry too, neither the one nor the other ever did any good. . . . Take his trumpery out of my sight."

Michelangelo's father didn't like his famous son's paintings; in fact they put him into a "violent rage." The artist saw his father thus transported with anger one day and said, "What an admirable subject for the pencil is my father in this fine passion!"

Picasso was such an object of rejection in his early days in Paris that one night when he got caught in the rain and asked an art dealer to let him bring in some paintings out of the wet the dealer wouldn't even give him, or them, shelter.

Picasso rather quickly overcame early rejection by sheer force of talent—many critics now
reckon that he was a genius, the greatest
painter of this century—and he spent the rest
of his long life turning out masterpieces born of
his own rejections, profound and productive,
first of the values of those who had rejected
him and then of all artistic creeds that were
static—did not deepen, widen, enlarge.

David Seymour/MAGNUM

One of the first to embrace impressionism,
he was one of the first to reject that movement,
because it had "lost all link with tradition" and
had not imposed enough compensatory discipline—"the kind of liberation that came in
with impressionism permitted every painter to
do what he wanted"—and without discipline
"painting was finished" and "sculpture died the
same death." To revive those arts (he was also
a very good sculptor) he began to experiment
with abstractions and started cubism, "the
manifestation of a vague desire . . . to get back
to some kind of order. . . ." Then he moved
on to a series of bewilderingly diverse, always
brilliant and arresting, always non-conformist
techniques.

Rejection of a thoroughly positive sort was
something that he valued deeply and wanted
others to share: "When I paint, I always try to
give an image people are not expecting . . .
one they reject. . . . I give a man an image of
himself . . . unexpected and disturbing enough
to make it impossible for him to escape the
questions it raises." (Most of those quotes are
from that remarkable book *Life With Picasso* by
Françoise Gilot and Carlton Lake.)

Perhaps the best known painted mother outside of religious art, Whistler's *Arrangement in
Gray and Black, No. 1: The Artist's Mother* (his
name for the portrait), spent her first nineteen
years being rejected, insulted, pawned, and ex-
patriated. The artist first sent the picture to the
Royal Academy, an august association of artists
to which he desperately wanted to be elected,
in 1872. An Academy committee thought it
worthless and relegated it to the "cellar of the
rejected," to quote Hesketh Pearson's *The Man
Whistler*. Then a powerful member, Sir William
Boxall, saw "picture by Whistler" in an inven-
tory and asked what and where it was. One
committee member said that it was "down
among the dead men," another called it "a
thing," and a third declared that it was "a con-
founded arrangement or symphony or something of the kind." Boxall was so angered that

he threatened to resign, and the "thing" was fetched up and hung on a wall—in a dark corner. Whistler never sent any more pictures to the Academy and was never elected to membership: "His individuality as an artist and his wit as a man were against him," says Pearson, "and he had to suffer the usual fate of genius when judged by talent." In 1878 he took the picture and pawned it for much-needed cash. Later he retrieved it for £50 and in 1883 exhibited it in Paris. In 1891 the French government bought it and made him, the prophet without honor in his own country (except that he wasn't English, he was an American from Lowell, Massachusetts) an officer in the Legion of Honor. His mother now hangs in the Louvre.

Thomas Sully's famous painting, *The Passage of the Delaware*, commonly called *Washington Crossing the Delaware*, was commissioned for $1000 by the state of North Carolina. But when it was finished, in 1819, it was rejected by that state because it was too big for the intended space in the capitol building. It is now in the Museum of Fine Arts in Boston.

Rembrandt's huge *Conspiracy of Julius Civilis* was hung in the Amsterdam town hall in July 1662 but soon thereafter removed, and it has never been returned to the lunette for which it was designed. Art historians reckon that it was "too brutal" for the serene classic taste of the age.

Mary Cassatt, *Lady at the Tea Table* (1885), oil on canvas; 29 × 24, The Metropolitan Museum of Art, gift of the artist, 1923.

Mrs. Robert Riddle, a relative of the artist Mary Cassatt, once gave her a blue-and-white tea set. In gratitude the artist painted a portrait of Mrs. Riddle seated at a table on which the set was prominently displayed. The portrait was a powerful study of a strong, controlled woman presiding like a priestess over the bright instruments of a graceful ritual, but Mrs. Riddle's daughter didn't like it; she thought the nose too big. Cassatt was so upset by the rejection that she put the picture in storage. That was in 1885. Not until 1914, when a friend saw it and persuaded her to exhibit it, was the *Lady at the Tea Table* seen again. Now it hangs in the Metropolitan Museum of Art in New York.

The most famous of all portrait rejections is one that never happened. In any discussion of the subject, especially among artists and cognoscenti, it is the example that is surest to be cited, and yet . . . .

As Seymour Slive, director of Harvard's Fogg Art Museum, writes in his authoritative book, *Rembrandt and His Critics,*

The Ur-myth on Rembrandt states that Rembrandt was a howling success . . . until 1642 when he painted the Night Watch, *a group portrait of . . . civic guards. . . . All Amsterdam was shocked, runs the tale. . . . The men who commissioned the painting were outraged. . . . Did they each pay Rembrandt one hundred guilders to be depicted as a dim piece of animated shade? No, this picture was unacceptable. . . .*

There was a tremendous scandal. . . . From 1642 until his death in 1669 Rembrandt received few, if any, commissions. The Night Watch *was cut down and hung on some obscure wall. . . .*

Rembrandt . . . spent his last years . . . without a friend or a guilder, or even a good piece of herring.

This . . . makes a wonderfully romantic story and perhaps it finds wide acceptance today because of the current belief that . . . any great artist must be misunderstood by his contemporaries.

Facts are, writes Slive, "It is true that Rembrandt's *Night Watch* broke many traditions of . . . Dutch group portrait painting, but there is absolutely no evidence to support the assumption that his patrons were dissatisfied with the picture, and that it caused a tremendous shift in his fortune. . . ."

Two of the guardsmen portrayed declared later that Rembrandt had been paid the full amount agreed on, 1600 guilders, for the "piece of painting." The portrait was never hung on an obscure wall—"It was in . . . a large new guild hall . . . until it was moved in 1715 to the Town Hall of Amsterdam"—and Rembrandt's supposed downward journey into poverty and oblivion simply "never took place," says Slive. Four years after he painted the *Night Watch* (which, by the way, was not given that name until late in the eighteenth century), Rembrandt was paid 2400 guilders for an *Adoration of the Shepherds* and a *Circumcision* that he painted for the royal court at The Hague.

A Rembrandt portrait was tentatively rejected once and the artist's response was not passive. In 1654 a Portuguese merchant named Diego Andrada testified to a notary that he had commissioned a portrait of a girl and given

Rembrandt a seventy-five-guilder deposit. After viewing the work in progress he was dissatisfied and ordered the painter to change it or return the deposit. Rembrandt refused. He said that he would show the picture to a group of fellow artists and if they thought it should be changed he would, otherwise not—and no refund of deposit. "And if this arrangement did not suit Andrada [quoting Slive again], the painter stated that he would finish the portrait at his convenience and sell it at auction." What happened next is not known, but the record shows that Rembrandt knew how to reject a would-be rejection.

According to his executors, Rubens painted a picture of the *Three Graces* for the Duke of Mantua but the artist's first wife hated the picture so much that it was sold to an agent of the King of England, who presumably wasn't so easily displeased.

Buildings and monuments suffer at the hands of rejection, too. Napoleon rejected the Carousel Triumphal Arch (now near the Louvre), erected solely for his glorification. "Take it away," he said, "and build me a real one." The result was the present colossal Arc de Triomphe.

*Build
Me
A
More
Stately . . .*

. . . Mansion!

The Royal Festival Hall, designed to be a main attraction of the 1951 Festival of Britain, was publicly despised. (It still is, although finicky Londoners say that they have suffered worse things since, notably the Post Office Tower and the National Theatre Building.)

One of the most successful expositions ever staged, Montreal's Expo 67, featured an ultramodern housing complex called Habitat, supposed to be *le dernier cri* in twentieth-century living. It was effusively gushed over in glossy journals and finally, with ruffles and flourishes, made available to renters. There were no renters. It was a monumental flop. Montrealers totally rejected it. It took ten years of frantic cajolery, and much rent reduction, to lure tenants in.

Moshe Safdie and Associates Inc.

Donato Bramante (1444–1514) so loved the architecture of the Greeks and the Romans that when he was commissioned by the Pope to design the church of St. Peter in Rome he dreamed of a vast square structure with chapels symmetrically clustered around a huge cross-shaped hall, the hall to be topped by a cupola resting on great arches. Since Christian tradition demanded oblong halls with the worshipers all looking eastward toward the main altar, there was opposition.

Then the huge structure devoured so much money that the Pope started the practice of selling indulgences to pay for it. That enraged many people, especially Martin Luther. His first public protest was made against it, and ultimately the opposition swelled into the Reformation.

Bramante

Bramante's plan was abandoned. All that he left to the St. Peter's of today was its enormous size.

The American architect Edgar Chambless designed a most ingenious city to be built like a shell around and along a highway. For nearly thirty years he tried to sell "Roadtown." People were interested, but. . . . One morning poor Edgar jumped out of his hotel room window.

The building originally proposed in 1952 for Boston's Back Bay Center, now known as Prudential Center, was turned down for the building that now stands there, the Prudential Tower. The rejected design was used for New York's Pan American Building.

Don't slam the door on your way out

Is it true that Boston's South Station was offered to the subway system and not accepted because the old landmark was home to too many pigeons?

Among the many ultra-novel ideas promulgated—but never sold—by that ultra-imaginative dreamer-doer Buckminster Fuller was one that could conceivably some day excite energy savers: a two-mile-diameter transparent dome poised over a city. "A dome over mid-Manhattan," declared Fuller, "would reduce its energy losses approximately fifty-fold."

An idea slightly more practical than Fuller's but just as rejectable was proposed by Canadian architect Oscar Newman in 1969. He suggested that since an atomic test in Nevada had produced "a perfect hollow sphere, a half-mile in diameter, five hundred feet below the earth," overpopulated cities like New York and Tokyo might consider using such holes in the ground for overflow habitations: "Manhattan could have half a dozen such atomic cities strung under the city proper . . . . The real problem in an underground city would be lack of view and fresh air, but consider its easy access to the surface and the fact that even as things are, our air should be filtered and what most of us see from our windows is somebody else's wall." It may well be that before the next century is over stranger ideas than that may be accepted, but its time is definitely not yet.

Sir John Vanbrugh (1664–1726) was a playwright as well as an architect and for a while was rejected in one field because of incompetence in the other. He designed an opera house in London especially for production of his own plays—the acoustics were so bad that the plays failed. (Not to worry. He went on to design that colossus of colossi, Blenheim Palace.)

Architectural rejections can be spectacular. In 1825 England's King George IV ordered architect John Nash to build a palace. The architect was old and tired; the king was old and tired and impatient. The work was rushed, and the result was a monstrosity. Buckingham Palace became such a laughingstock that Nash was cross-examined by a select committee, and after the king's death in 1830 he was dismissed. The next king, William IV ("Silly Billy"), had no use for the pile. Not until his niece, Victoria, found it convenient was the palace accepted as a royal residence.

BUCKINGHAM PALACE.

The same thing happened, in a not quite royal way, in California, to the 1.3 million-dollar governor's mansion in a posh residential section of Sacramento. Begun when Ronald Reagan was governor, it was completed after Jerry Brown took office, and he called it "the Taj Mahal" and rejected it. He preferred to live in a simple apartment across the street from the capitol (and to sleep, rumor had it, on the floor).

When Derek Bok became president of Harvard he chose to live in a private house in Cambridge rather than in the official presidential residence in the college yard.

Isn't it true that not too long ago in a western state (Montana?) an entire U.S. Army base was authorized, constructed, and declared ready for occupancy by one part of the army (Corps of Engineers?), and then, by some other part of that same army (Quartermaster Corps?), rejected?

One of this country's greatest architects was also one of the most rejected—and rejecting. Frank Lloyd Wright denounced all sorts of things, including Gibbon's *Decline and Fall of the Roman Empire* ("the habitual"), education ("creeping paralysis"), business ("sinister"—realtor equals "lousy bastard"), Christianity ("spirit betrayed"), the Renaissance ("asinine"), Michelangelo ("unluckily, painted pictures of sculpture"), London ("full of pathetic charm" but "senile"), New York ("greatest mouth"), the whole Western world ("glorified hypocrisy").

Jun Fujita/Chicago Historical Society (ICHI-12960)

(What did he like? Music, truth, work, Plutarch's *Lives*, Japanese houses ("honest," "nothing meaningless"), "faith and rebellion," all "true" creations, including his own and Beethoven's—"when [he] made music I am sure he . . . saw buildings . . . like mine.")

As an architect he was so wildly original that orthodox critics were forever lambasting him, and he always gave as good as, or better than, he got. He said that his fellow architects were "parasitic . . . unable to do more than band together to protect themselves." They were not "creators" but only "operators," and they turned out "shabby finery"—public buildings which were "mediocre" and private dwellings which were "a general fiasco," looking as if "cut from cardboard." Wright once met the noted architect Philip Johnson at a party and said, "Philip, are you still building those little houses and leaving them out in the rain?"

Wright regarded his own designs as all but divinely inspired, although large numbers of them never left the drawing board, and his pronouncements concerning their detractors seemed to fall as from a great height, like ecclesiastical anathemas or writs of excommunication. Jonathan Swift once wrote, "When a true genius appears in the world, you may know him by this sign, that the dunces are all in confederacy against him." Wright reckoned that he was a living demonstration of that—he wrote a book called *Genius and the Mobocracy*.

Ayn Rand's immensely popular novel *The Fountainhead* (rejected many times before it was finally published in 1943) featuring a belligerent architect who blows up his building rather than let the soulless money-grubbers (who have paid for it) mess up its pure lines, was inspired by Wright. (He did fulminate loudly against many buildings and changes of design but he never blew up a building.)

One of Wright's last designs was also one of his most ambitious. Proposed in 1956, the "Mile-High Skyscraper" was just that, a needle-like building soaring 528 storeys into the air. It was to have four four-lane approach roads and two landing pads for fifty helicopters each, covered parking for 15,000 cars and office space for 130,000 people, "in spacious comfort." The fifty-six elevators run by atomic power plus some escalators "should fill or empty the entire building within the hour." (Words Wright's.)

Needless to say the Mile-High never got off the ground. Not because it wasn't feasible; it was. It was just too challenging.

And that, ultimately, was also its designer's grief and glory. Wright was too challenging. It was hard to see him clearly because he was so outsized, his visions so shining, his affirmations

Chicago Historical Society
(ICHI-00079)

and rejections so overpowering. As Voltaire said of Napoleon, "Voilà un homme!"

It seems that the most terrible rejection that Frank Lloyd Wright ever suffered was delivered to him, though not directly, by a servant. In 1914 he was living in what was then called sin with a woman who wasn't his wife in his famous house "Taliesin" in Spring Green, Wisconsin. On August 15 while he was away on a trip, his butler, Julian Carleton, burned the house and axe-murdered the woman, her two children, and four other people who happened to be there. Carleton, who was noted for his strict morals, died in jail after swallowing acid so that he could not testify, and although he stated that he had acted to revenge himself on a draftsman who had insulted him, it was, and is, generally believed that his real motive was violent disapproval of his master's behavior.

It seems people, too, get rejected, oftentimes fatally, more often blithely, for their beliefs and their actions. Eight years before Wright's tragedy, another eminent American architect had suffered the ultimate moral rejection. Stanford White, designer of many stately civic buildings, dallied with pretty Evelyn Nesbit, called by the newspapers of the time "the girl in the red velvet swing," who happened to be the wife of his friend Harry K. Thaw.

On June 25, 1906, Thaw shot the dallier to death.

(Thaw, an eccentric—to say the least—millionaire, then spent some time in a mental hospital. When he was at large again he saw one of the Palm Beach gingerbred-gothic palaces designed by Addison Mizner and said, "My God! I shot the wrong architect!")

When Newport was Newport (and not just a slightly misshapen microcosm of Megalopolis) the Coogan family of Coogan's Bluff fame bought a cottage, moved in, and issued invitations to a gala. Ignorant of high society mores, the poor clods didn't append the required R.S.V.P. Naturally nobody, simply nobody, my dear, came. Next day the Coogans sold their house and moved back to Brooklyn. *Rejector,* as Carlyle might have said, *rejectus.*

Jesus rejected rejecters.

"And the scribes and Pharisees brought unto

him a woman taken in adultery [and said]
Moses in the law commanded . . . that such
should be stoned . . . what sayest thou? [Jesus
said] He that is without sin among you, let him
first cast a stone. . . ."

Socrates was condemned to death by his fellow Athenians because he persisted in instruct-
ing ("corrupting," the judges called it) the
youth.

The Liberace Museum,
Las Vegas

One the most glittering rejections-of-rejec-
tion of the entire twentieth century has been
credited to that be-sequined, candle-lit, piano-
caressing showoff Wladziu Valentino Liberace.
Asked how he felt about the rich stream of ridicule that poured over him when he started
making it big with the Lawrence Welk set in
the 1950s ("sentimental vomit," "triumph of
mediocrity," "nausea"), he is said to have said,
"I cried all the way to the bank." Actually
what he said was, "My brother George and I
laughed all the way to the bank." The number
of times he had to make that trip he could have
done both and sung a little on the side.

All of the loud ridicule didn't hurt Liberace as much as the silent rejection of his music by one man—his father. Salvatore Liberace came to this country from Italy, taught himself to play the French horn and the trumpet, and performed with John Philip Sousa's marching band and the Milwaukee Philharmonic. He so despised his son's fooling around that for years he couldn't bring himself even to speak of the *guzzabuglio stomachevole* ("disgusting mess"). Only late in life would he admit that maybe, perhaps, crazy Wladziu might be, in his own lousy way, something of a success.

Liberace himself has always been an easygoing fellow. When he was just getting started with a band he was offered a chance to play with the Chicago Symphony—on condition that he not use the same name in the orchestra that he used in the band. Those classical musicians felt about pop music just as Salvatore did. "So I told the bandleader to call me anything but Liberace, and he came up with Walter Busterkeys." Busterkeys!

And Busterkeys it was.

After more years than it takes to grow a cornfed beauty from cradle to girdle, Bert Parks was summarily fired from his job of master of all of the Miss Americas.

Sic *Gloria* *Transit*

G.K. Chesterton, eminent British writer, was an obese and unpopular child and couldn't read until he was eight. One of his masters said that if his head were opened "we should not find any brain but only a lump of white fat."

Winston Churchill failed the entrance exams to Sandhurst twice before he finally passed.

The Ashmolean Museum, Oxford

Emile Zola failed the Sorbonne exams in language and literature—he forgot the date of Charlemagne's death (814, of course), botched German reading, and messed up a simple fable. Later he tried to enter the University of Marseilles and failed the written exams so miserably that he didn't even take the orals.

Thomas A. Edison's first teacher called him "addled," and other educators promised that he would "never make a success of anything."

As a boy one of the finest thinkers of the Middle Ages, philosopher-theologian-scientist-writer Saint Albertus Magnus was rated an utter dolt by his Dominican teachers and declared incapable of serious study.

Edgar Allan Poe was thrown out of West Point and so was Whistler.

Gregor Mendel, founder of genetics, was rejected by his university. He went to the University of Vienna but left without graduating. One of his professors wrote, "Mendel lacks the requisite clarity of thought to be a scientist."

Giacomo Puccini's music teacher said he had no talent and gave up on him.

Einstein's parents feared that he was retarded and a teacher told him he would never amount to anything.

Between the ages of six and sixteen, Gamal Abdel Nasser passed only four grades.

Scottish engineer James Watt was a lifelong victim of migraine headaches; as a child he was bullied and called "dull and inept."

Arthur Wellesley, Duke of Wellington, was such a bad student that his mother took him out of Eton and finally pushed him into a military career, saying that he was "fit food for [cannon] powder."

As a youth Adolf Hitler (né Schicklgruber—and if he had not rejected that name could he have gone on to command fear?) suffered four artistic rejections. He tried to enter the Academy of Fine Arts in Vienna and was rejected because his test drawing was unsatisfactory. The next year he tried again and was not even allowed to take the entrance examination. He was rejected by the School of Architecture because he lacked the required high school diploma. He submitted a painting to the Academy for exhibition and it was rejected: "Adolf stormed back to inquire who composed the jury. Among them was a Jew, a recognized authority on art. Hitler blamed the jury's negative verdict on the Jew and declared the Jewish people 'shall pay for this.' "

Trojan Paris rejected the goddesses of power and wisdom for the goddess of love, got Greek Helen, and started the Trojan War, the wanderings of Ulysses, and much of our modern mythology.

The seeds of a hundred novels were sown when Joseph rejected Potiphar's wife, and another thousand when young Cleopatra did *not* reject old Caesar, and a thousand thousand psychic studies when Oedipus was rejected by his father and Cinderella by her mother (stepmother, actually—psychologists prefer the term "mother figures." And they say that real or fancied rejection of children by their parents is one of the most powerful forces in character molding).

Joseph rejecting Potiphar's wife

Athena, goddess of wisdom, rejected all men. The Christian saints rejected all women. Narcissus rejected everybody, and so, for different reasons and with different results, did Timon of Athens and Nero of Rome.

One of the best-loved of all romantic rejections graces (*mot juste*) the pages of *Pride and Prejudice*. Mr. Darcy condescendingly informs Elizabeth that she may have his hand. She gives him the back of hers: "From the very beginning . . . of my acquaintance with you, your manners, impressing me with the fullest belief of your arrogance, your conceit, and your self-ish disdain of the feelings of others, were such as to form that groundwork of disapprobation on which succeeding events have built so immovable a dislike; and I had not known you a month before I felt that you were the last man in the world whom I could ever be prevailed on to marry."

One of our two favorite early American ladies rejected the man who proposed to her and accepted one who didn't. Colonial Governor Miles Standish was too haughty or timid or something to woo Priscilla Mullins in person so he sent his friend John Alden to ask her hand in marriage. The messenger delivered the message honorably and so attractively that although he had said nothing about any feelings he might have had for her Priscilla said to him, "Speak for yourself, John." John did. Poor Miles!

The second of those ladies, Pocahontas, rejected her Indian heritage to marry Captain John Smith.

National Portrait Gallery, Smithsonian Institution, Washington, D.C., gift of Andrew W. Mellon (NPG 65.51)

Henry VIII was a wife rejecter. He divorced Catherine of Aragon, beheaded Anne Boleyn, divorced Anne of Cleves, beheaded Catherine Howard, and probably would have beheaded or divorced Catherine Parr if he had lived long enough—he married her in 1542 and died in 1547. (His third wife, Jane Seymour, died after giving birth to the future Edward VI.) When he was shopping around for a fourth wife he was shown a picture of Anne of Cleves and waved her away as a "Flanders mare," so he almost rejected her twice. She survived rejection, and rejecter, very well—divorced after being married only six months in 1540, she was pensioned and lived happily ever after or at least until her death, from natural causes, in 1557.

"The greatest number of marriages in the monogamous world is nineteen, by Mr. Glynn de Moss Wolf (U.S.) (b. 1908)," says the 1978 *Guinness Book of World Records,* noting that Mrs. Beverly Nina Avery of Los Angeles "set a monogamous world record in October 1957 by obtaining her sixteenth divorce. . . ." She may not always have been the more active rejecter—she said that five of her husbands had broken her nose. The notorious Tommy Manville was married only thirteen times, once for a total of 7½ hours.

Newton

Ruskin

John Ruskin, English reformer, essayist, and art critic utterly rejected sex, and was himself partially rejected by Nature. Literary sex was all right—as warmly as the singer of *The Song of Solomon,* he wrote of "snowy mountains and sweet valleys"—but when he married his beloved and saw her pubic hair he was so shocked that he remained a virgin for the rest of his long life (1819–1900). He was obsessed by sex, kept a diary of his sex thoughts, was mentally and emotionally unstable, and during his last 22 years suffered bouts of insanity.

So did Isaac Newton live and die a virgin.

And so may have Adolf Hitler, supposed to have had only one testicle.

Poor rich Howard Hughes started off by liking sex and people in small doses. His appetite, or tolerance, for both of those doses got smaller and smaller until, like the oysters who walked with the Walrus and the Carpenter, "there were none"—and only a pitiful shred of him.

Poor poor fellow! All that money and power, and no love—to give or to receive.

More (some?) rejection in childhood and early manhood might have taught him the joy of acceptance and sharing.

Hell hath no fury like a woman scorned. After Potiphar's wife had almost raped Joseph— "she caught him by his garment, saying, Lie with me; and he left his garment in her hand, and fled"—she claimed that he had attacked her, and he was thrown into jail.

Medea helped Jason kill the dragon guarding the Golden Fleece, betrayed her father, killed her brother, and fled with Jason and bore him two sons. He rejected her for a princess. She sent the princess a beautiful robe, which burned her to ashes, then she killed her two sons and flew away.

If the Puritans hadn't rejected and been rejected by the Church of England and then rejected the whole of the Old World, where, and who, would our WASPiest of WASPs be today?

Fogg Art Museum, Harvard University, Gift of Grenville L. Winthrop, Pierre Narcisse Guerin, Hippolytus and Phaedra, 1949.191

After six months in a California convent Jane Cahill joined IBM, worked her way up to vice-president, married Ralph Pfeiffer, Jr., refused an offer from President Carter to be Secretary of Commerce, and became the $225,000-per-year chairman of NBC. She also earned for herself the title Attila the Nun.

In February 1953 actress June Haver entered St. Mary's convent in Xavier, Kansas. Seven months later she left the convent, complaining of migraine headaches. In 1954 she married actor Fred MacMurray.

The beautiful boy Hippolytus rejected his stepmother Phaedra—and his father Theseus obviously didn't like it. According to one version of the myth Phaedra, like Potiphar's wife, lied about the affair and told Theseus that Hippolytus had pursued her. Theseus then caused a bull to kill his son.

Hippolytus
& Co.

Rejection, like resurrection, can outlive death. Pope Formosus died in 896. A successor, Stephen VII, hated him so much in life that although he was, as Joseph S. Brusher's book *Popes Through The Ages* puts it, "dead and buried with honor. . . . This last fact could still be cancelled." Eight months after burial, the body of Formosus was dug up, clothed in the papal robes, and propped in a witness chair. There ensued a "cadaveric synod"—Formosus's body was tried for misdeeds in office. Stephen served as prosecutor and a deacon represented the defendant. The verdict was guilty, the corpse was stripped of its robes—underneath was found a hair shirt—and the three fingers used in the papal blessing were cut off. The body was then buried in a pilgrims' cemetery, but a gang dug it up and threw it into the Tiber.

Thomas à Becket, archbishop of Canterbury, was murdered by four knights in 1170. Two years later the martyr-rebel was canonized, and his influence grew even greater than it had been in life. In 1538 Henry VIII of England had his skeleton brought before the Star Chamber and tried for usurpation of papal authority. Verdict: guilty. The bones were burned in a public bonfire "to admonish the living of their duty"—to the crown.

Soon-to-be-rejected Wycliffe

In 1415 the Council of Constance declared the English religious reformer John Wycliffe, dead since 1384, a heretic. In 1428 his bones were dug up, burned, and scattered.

"For a just man falleth seven times, and riseth up again. . . ." —Proverbs 24:16

For Joan of Arc it was the other way around. Rejection came during life; trial, and acquittal, later.

Abandoned by her people and Charles VII, the king whom she had crowned, she was sentenced to death by the Church and burned in Rouen in 1431. Twenty-four years later the king appointed three bishops to reopen the case—but not the coffin. The court decided that the previous action had been an "atrocious miscarriage of justice." In 1920 the Maid was canonized.

When Martin Bormann, war-time Nazi official, was tried by the Nuremberg War Crimes prosecutor in 1946, he was not present, and it was not known whether he was living or dead. He was convicted anyway and sentenced to be hung. Not possible. In 1972 his grave was discovered by workmen at a Berlin construction site—he had been dead since 1945.

It is axiomatic that a scientific discovery that is too far ahead of its time is rejected or ignored. Gregor Mendel discovered the gene in 1865; not until the turn of the century was that discovery generally accepted. Friedrich Miescher found deoxyribonucleic acid (DNA) in the cell nucleus in 1869, and his discovery was ignored until 1944, when Oscar Avery went on to show that DNA was a genetic agent; Avery's finding was similarly ignored until 1953, when James Watson and Francis Crick demonstrated that DNA's double helix was the actual genetic carrier, the discovery for which they won the Nobel Prize in Medicine and Physiology. Between 1914 and 1916 Michael Polanyi put forward a theory that the attraction of solid surfaces for gas molecules depends on the position of the molecules and not on electrostatic forces. In those days it was popularly believed that that attraction *did* involve electrostatic forces, and "in spite of the fact that Polanyi was able to provide strong experimental evidence in favor of his theory, it was generally rejected," as molecular geneticist Gunther Stent reported in an article in the December 1972 issue of *Scientific American* magazine. "Not only was the theory rejected, it was also considered so ridiculous by the leading authorities of the time that Polanyi believes continued defense of his theory would have ended his professional career if he had not managed to publish work on more palatable ideas. [His theory was] consigned so authoritatively to the ashcan of crackpot ideas that it was rediscovered only in the 1950s."

In his article Dr. Stent wondered why scientists so consistently reject theories that are ahead of their time, and he came to an interesting conclusion: by the subtle operation known as "structuralism," conclusively demonstrated in recent neurophysiological experiments with higher mammals, information "enters the mind not as raw data but in already highly abstracted form, namely as structures," and in the creation of these structures, or recognizable patterns, concepts incompatible with already existing ideas are selectively destroyed. That is, the unconscious part of the brain processes incoming information and filters out incongruous ideas before they reach the conscious mind: " . . . a discovery cannot be appreciated until it can be connected logically to contemporary canonical knowledge." So the decision to reject a novel idea is made subconsciously.

Dr. Stent thinks that structural blockage is still at work among scientists, and cites two examples of recently claimed discoveries that may be "premature at this very time." One is the "alleged finding" that the "engram, or memory trace, of a task learned by a trained animal can be transferred to a naive animal by injection or feeding the recipient with an extract made from the tissues of the donor." The experiments involved have been difficult to repeat "and the results claimed for them may indeed not be true at all [structuralist thinking, Dr. Stent?] " . . . It is nonetheless significant that few neurophysiologists have even bothered to check these experiments, even though . . . the possibility of chemical memory transfer would constitute a fact of capital importance." The other is the "troublesome subject of ESP, or extrasensory perception." Dr. Stent feels that while there may be merit in the theory of ESP, further experiments such as those with cards of J. B. Rhine at Duke University or even new ones involving, possibly, molecular beams that might be affected by mental activity would be futile now, because "any positive evidence . . . found in favor of ESP would be . . . premature. That is, until it is possible to connect ESP with canonical knowledge of, say, electromagnetic radiation and neurophysiology, no demonstration of its occurrence could be appreciated."

Sometimes rejections are foolhardy . . .

Spallanzani

In 1793 the renowned Italian naturalist Lazzaro Spallanzani determined by experiment that bats can avoid obstacles while flying with their eyes sealed. At the same time a Swiss surgeon, Louis Jurine, found that if bats' ears were sealed the animals have difficulty navigating. Spallanzani experimented until the evidence that bats rely on their ears more than their eyes for "seeing" was conclusive. He never published his findings, but word of them got around and stirred derisive comment: "Do bats hear with their eyes, then?"

The establishment continued to cling to the theory that bats' amazing ability to navigate in the dark was due to some kind of touch.

In 1920 a British acoustics expert suggested that the navigating mechanism might be acoustic, and in the late 1930s two Harvard students, Donald Griffin and Robert Galambos, working with caged bats and high-frequency sound pulses, proved that bats use sound more than sight for obstacle and prey detection.

Time between discovery and acceptance: 147 years.

"The speculation . . . is interesting, but the impossibility of ever doing it is so certain that it is not practically useful." —Editor of Popular Astronomy *in a rejection letter to rocket pioneer Robert Goddard, who had proposed consideration of nuclear energy, 1902*

Engineer Frank Whittle offered a jet engine to the British Government in 1923. Not until 1939 did jet engines go into production.

"Flight by machines heavier than air is unpractical and insignificant, if not utterly impossible." —SIMON NEWCOMB, *eminent astronomer, eighteen months before the Wright brothers flew*

An instrument for studying the electric waves generated by the brain was built in Germany in the 1890s and not put to use until 1934.

George B. Selden invented the modern gas-powered automobile in 1877 and spent the next fifteen years trying to get it manufactured.

"Rail travel at high speed is not possible, because passengers, unable to breathe, would die of asphyxia." —DR. DIONYSUS LARDNER (1793–1859), *professor of natural philosophy and astronomy at University College, London. Dr. Lardner also said that no large steamship could ever cross the Atlantic, two years before the Great Western did.*

Smithsonian Institution, Washington, D.C.

In 1714 Queen Anne of England granted her subject Henry Mills a patent for a machine that wrote. The machine didn't write very much. Years went by, and more than fifty other inventors invented machines that wrote, but not well enough. In 1874 Mark Twain saw a girl demonstrating one, called a *Type-Writer*. On it she could type more than fifty words a minute. He bought "this curiosity-breeding little joker" and on it typed—at nineteen words a minute—*Life on the Mississippi*. But 35 more years had to pass before Type-Writing machines fell into—under—the hands of people everywhere.

Jean-Jacques Perret of France invented a guard to make razor blades "safe" in 1762. In 1904, King Camp Gillette of the United States patented the first safety razor with thin, sharp, disposable blades, while William Nickerson designed machinery for commercial production. The experts had all told Gillette that such thin sharp blades couldn't be made; said he, "If I had been technically trained, I would have quit."

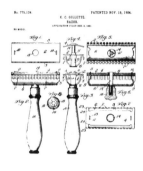

The Gillette Company

That invaluable compendium of crucial information, *The Book of Lists #1*, has this round-up of long time intervals between concepts and realizations:

Antibiotics 1910–1940   *Radar 1904–1939*

Frozen foods 1908–1923   *Radio 1890–1914*

Heart pacemaker 1928–1960   *Silicone 1904–1942*

Helicopter 1904–1941   *Television 1884–1947*

Nuclear energy 1919–1965   *Zipper 1883–1913*

Photography 1782–1838

Rejection by inaction can be costly.

John Ericsson of Sweden invented a fire engine that was doing a good job of putting out fires in the 1830s. It pumped two tons of water a minute. Firemen hated it because it threatened their jobs, and persuaded a mob to destroy it.

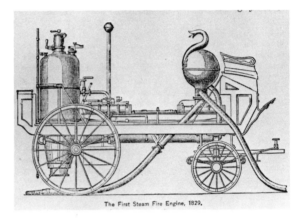

The First Steam Fire Engine, 1829.

"We hope that Professor Langley will not put his substantial greatness as a scientist in further peril by continuing to waste his time and the money involved, in further airship experiments. Life is too short. . . ."
—The New York Times editorial, 1903

" . . . physically impossible for pilot to withstand a speed much over 400 miles per hour. . . ." —Dr. Starr Truscott, *aeronautical engineer for the National Advisory Committee for Aeronautics, 1929*

In 1826 a Scot, the Rev. Patrick Bell, demonstrated a device for cutting wheat by scissoring it between moving blades on metal strips. Farm laborers destroyed it.

Cyrus McCormick patented his soon-to-be-essential reaper in 1834. He was wiped out in the panic of 1837 and creditors could have taken that patent but didn't because they didn't think it was worth the trouble.

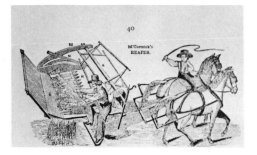

When rifle sights were first provided to the British Army during the Napoleonic wars, an officer commanding Irish troops tried to reject them because, he said, if his men were given them every English landlord in Ireland would be dead in two weeks.

Charles Goodyear failed in the hardware business and as a maker of rubber bags for the Postal Service, spent time in debtor's prison, sold his children's schoolbooks—and invented vulcanized rubber.

McCormick

Thomas Edison rejected the help of a hearing aid because he found noises distracting, and "my wife would want to talk to me all the time."

The MIT Museum and Historical Collections

When the infant Bell telephone company was struggling to get started, its owners offered all of their rights to the established Western Union Company for $100,000. WU President Orton said "What use could this company make of an electrical toy?" and rejected the offer.

The MIT Museum and Historical Collections

> *"The thing that hath been, it is that which shall be; and that which is done is that which shall be done: and there is no new thing under the sun."* —*Ecclesiastes* 1:9

In 1934 Chrysler brought out the first streamlined automobile, the Airflow. Critics ridiculed its novel appearance, especially the "round blandness" and "rhinocerine ungainliness" of its "bug-eyed" front end, which they compared to a "face covered with a stocking." Initial demand was small, and the pioneer gave up and scrubbed the model. Other car makers were quick to profit from it: in 1936 Ford introduced its somewhat similarly designed Lincoln Zephyr and Volkswagen came out with the Beetle. General Motors followed with the "Fastback." O market courage, O parlor rejection, O loss of nerve! Chrysler bought the future and gave it away.

Did the British spurn the chance to take over Volkswagen after World War II?

'Twas ever thus. Whatever became of Leonardo da Vinci's carefully worked out, within-the-state-of-the-art, gadgets for making peace more prosperous, war more decisive? Or those of Roger Bacon, two centuries earlier? Or those of the Greek engineers, uninteresting to Plato and his philosopher friends? Rejection by pocket veto can be more effective than that by public vote. Ancient Mesopotamians and Egyptians and their successors rode around in chariots but it took the cathedral builders to make a wheel-

barrow—surely, in all of those thousands of years, somebody thought of putting the wheel to that kind of work? At this moment, how many space-age marvels lie in the Patent Office like sleeping beauties waiting for a kiss that will never come?

Edison rejected pretty nearly everything except his inventions, the making of them, and the success that came from them. He drove his workers like cattle and neglected his family. Both of his wives suffered severe depressions and his oldest son killed himself.

Edison even rejected sleep. He got along on about three hours a night and thought that was too much.

In 1890 Edison was asked to collaborate on an imaginative novel about the future, to be titled *Progress*. He wrote down some predictions for the mid-twentieth century: plastics, airplanes, journeys to Mars, apes that could be taught to speak English. Then he lost interest and rejected the whole idea.

Is it true that in 1912 Thomas Edison and Nicola Tesla were offered the Nobel Prize jointly for their work in electricity, and that Tesla said he wouldn't share anything with a "mechanic," so neither got the prize, which went to a Swede named Nils Dalen, inventor of automatic gas regulators for use in lighthouses, buoys, and railway lights?

> *"Fooling around with alternating current is just a waste of time."*
> —Thomas Edison

The men who are supposed to make this age great, our giants of industry, are not always giants of intellect. Kodak was offered Chester Carlson's patent on xerography and saw nothing worthwhile in it. A half dozen other firms also rejected the patent before Haloid picked it up and formed the Xerox Corporation.

One of the other firms that turned down the xerography patent was IBM—on the advice of the highly esteemed market analysis company, Arthur D. Little.

J. Murray Forbes, one of bygone Boston's most eminent citizens, once heard that a "young man, down in Salem, named Bell" had invented a thing which he called a "telephone." Forbes investigated, and concluded that the transmission of sound was not by a wire, as claimed, but by "some fellow hidden on the roof with some kind of horn." He laughed and refused to invest. Then he heard that another inventor, named Edison, was saying that he "could light by electricity a room and even a whole town." Forbes again investigated, and laughed some more. "I did not think the device amounted to a row of pins. . . .".

In 1887 a salesman named Richard Sears and a watchmaker named Alvah Roebuck, who had only been earning $3.50 per week plus room and board, started a new company in Chicago—not a big company to begin with, but promising. Sears, Roebuck became the largest mail-order business in the country, despite an astonishing series of rejections and un-rejec-

Sears

Roebuck

tions by one or the other of the two founders—for thirty years they bounced out of and back into their creation like yo-yos.

First the infant company got into money trouble and Sears resigned. Two months later he came back. Then he resigned again, apparently for good—he sold out to Roebuck. This time he was back in a week. (And he stayed on until he retired in 1908.)

Then it was Roebuck's turn. By 1895 the company was grossing $800,000 a year but netting very little. Roebuck said, "I have had enough" (meaning that he didn't have enough), and he sold out to Sears for $25,000. Unwise. Four years later Roebuckless Sears was grossing $8½ million a year and netting a lot.

Roebuck stayed on for four more years (without partnership perks) and finally quit permanently (he thought), and started a company of his own, making movie projectors.

His company prospered; he sold it for $150,000, went into real estate in Florida, and was wiped out in 1929.

He came crawling back to a Searsless Roebuckless Sears, Roebuck and Co. in 1933 and worked on corporate odds and ends (including an early history of the company) until he retired—as a salaried employee—in 1940.

He died in 1948 at the age of eighty-four, not much richer than he had been at age twenty-three but maybe—who knows?—a little wiser.

Moral: don't quit even when you're not ahead.

Some things have never been rejected because they were never seriously considered. For instance, these inventions, all awarded patents by the U.S. Patent Office at various times, are only a few of the abundant harvest reaped by A. E. Brown and H. A. Jeffcott, Jr., in their revelating little book, *Absolutely Mad Inventions.*

Eye-protectors for chickens

Badge made of candy ("in no way destroys the confectionery, and may be disposed of in the usual manner for confectionery. . . .)"

"Combined grocer's package, grater, slicer, and mouse and fly trap"

Chewing gum locket ("anti-corrosive lining")

Tapeworm trap ("baited, attached to a string, and swallowed")

Saluting device ("elevation and rotation of the hat . . . by mechanism therein")

Method of preserving the dead ("within a block of transparent glass")

Improvement in fire escapes ("parachute . . . in combination with overshoes having elastic bottom pads of suitable thickness")

"Young man, you can be grateful that my invention is not for sale, for it would undoubtedly ruin you. It can be exploited for a certain time as a scientific curiosity, but apart from that it has no commercial value whatsoever." —AUGUSTE LUMIÈRE, *commenting on moving pictures, 1895*

In the 1830s when announcements of the discoveries of the Frenchmen Niepce and Daguerre heralded the arrival of photography, the Leipzig *City Advertiser* dismissed the absurd notion as typically Gallic bombast: "To fix fleeting reflections is not only impossible as has been shown by thorough-going German research, but to wish to do it is blasphemy."

"It will never be possible to synchronize the voice with the pictures. . . . There will never be speaking pictures."
—D.W. GRIFFITH, *1924*

"Who the hell wants to hear actors talk?
—H.M. WARNER, *date undetermined*

"Americans require a restful quiet in the moving picture theater, and for them talking . . . on the screen destroys the illusion. Devices for projecting the film actor's speech can be prefaced, but the idea is not practical." —THOMAS EDISON, *1926*

Clarence Saunders, founder of the South's famous Piggly Wiggly stores, pigwiggled through several gaudy rejections. First (1919) his directors talked him into Piggly Wiggly out of a name he suggested: Flopsy Wopsy. Then he was unhorsed on Wall street and kicked out of Piggly Wiggly. He started another chain, Clarence Saunders, Sole Owner of My Name, Stores, Inc., prospered, bought a Sole Owner football team, and went bankrupt. He started yet another store, named Keedoozle, and was planning another chain, to be called Lady Honor, when he wiggled his last, in 1953.

"The problem with television is that the people must sit and keep their eyes glued to a screen: the average American family hasn't time for it. Therefore the showmen are convinced that for this reason, if no other, television will never be a serious competitor of broadcasting." —The New York Times, March 1939

A Quaker named Walter Hunt was one of the nineteenth century's most capable inventors, but he never prospered very much financially because of his religion.

He made his first invention, a machine for spinning flax and hemp, in 1826. After that he developed a stove that could burn hard coal, a sort of a fountain pen, the first explosive gun cartridge, a repeating rifle, and a paper collar. In 1832 he put together a machine that could sew, stitch, and seam cloth—a sewing machine. By 1838 he had developed his idea to

Hunt

the point where he was ready to go into business manufacturing sewing machines in quantity.

Then he heard that machines that did humans' work took jobs away from humans—and
he walked away from the whole idea.

In 1854 Elias Howe, untroubled by scruples,
patented the first sewing machine.

In 1849 Hunt found himself owing $15 to a
friend; he started twisting a wire—and in three
hours he had twisted the wire into a device that
came to be known as a "safety pin." The friend
gave him $400 for the rights to the invention.

Most inventors at one time or another have
to fight off shrewd sharks who would like to buy
them out. With Walter Hunt it was the other
way around—he could hardly wait to abandon
projects that might have made his fortune.

King Menelaus of
Sparta hears
that his Queen,
Helen, has run
off to Troy with
Paris. (Water-
color by
Daumier).

Medical rejection can be the worst of all. It can result in unnecessary pain, malfunction, or death. The English physician Alexander Fleming published a report on the anti-bacteria powers of penicillin in 1929 but nothing was done about it until there came an urgent need to treat the wounded of World War II.

Jenner

In 1796 Edward Jenner proved conclusively that vaccination with serum taken from a dairymaid suffering from cowpox, a mild disease, gave protection against smallpox, a virulent one. He wrote a paper demonstrating his finding and sent it to the Royal Society. The Society rejected his paper, on the grounds that to publish it would damage the good reputation that Jenner had gained by his previous researches on cuckoos.

William Harvey published his epochal *de Motu Cordis et Sanguinis* ("of the Motion of the Heart and Blood"), proving that the heart pumps the blood through the body, in 1628. Many of his colleagues rejected his conclusion. One of them, French anatomist Jean Riolan, called him a quack, and others declared that even if he was correct they preferred to err with the ancients—who had believed that the heart's only function was to think and feel—rather than to be right with him.

Harvey

"Who shall decide, when doctors disagree. . . ?" —ALEXANDER POPE, *Moral Essays*

Indians had known about the pain-killing and tranquilizing powers of a certain plant for hundreds or thousands of years when a German, Leonard Rauwolf, "discovered" them in the sixteenth century. Nothing happened; nobody was helped (outside of India).

Came World War II with armies of wounded, and the virtues of that plant were discovered all over again, by Germans.

The plant is now officially named *rauwolfia*.

The classic example of bad medical rejection is the hard-to-believe case of Ignaz Philipp Semmelweiss and childbed fever.

Semmelweiss was a Hungarian physician practicing in a Vienna hospital when he determined, by thorough investigation and experi-

ment, that childbed fever, then much more prevalent in Vienna hospitals than in homes, could be caused by infection carried on doctors' hands.

In 1847 he ordered the doctors under him to wash their hands in strong chemicals before touching patients. The incidence of childbed fever fell dramatically. But in 1849 a Hungarian revolt against Austria was crushed and the Viennese doctors forced their Hungarian annoyer out. They went back to leaving their hands unwashed, and the incidence of childbed fever rose.

Semmelweiss went to a hospital in Budapest and again insisted that doctors wash their hands and again the incidence of childbed fever fell.

But the Viennese doctors were still not impressed and would not wash their hands. (They were proud of their "hospital odor.")

The circumstances of Semmelweiss' death were tragic and ironic. After nearly twenty years of struggling against the folly of his colleagues, he went mad, and in July 1865 was committed to an insane asylum. He had a cut in his hand when he treated his last patients, and in the next month he died of childbed fever.

> **"An idea born before its time must die—and often take its father with it."**
> —*Anthropological precept*

A recent do-it-yourself slimming book, *The Beverly Hills Diet,* became a bestseller but was rejected almost unanimously by nutritionists. They labeled it "ludicrous," "poppycock." Responding to her critics the author, Judy Mazel, said on national television that, "They laughed at Madame Curie when she said wash your hands and you'll kill bacteria." Of course it was Semmelweiss who said that. Curie's hands were probably black most of the time—she spent her life picking grains of radium out of tons of ore.

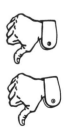

"*It's broccoli, dear.*"
"*I say it's spinach, and I say the hell with it.*"

Nor is the military exempt from rejection. Somebody once said that commanders always plan for, and if left to themselves fight, the last war. They are invincible rejecters of new ideas. Remember Billy Mitchell trying to sell airpower in 1921? Eight of his primitive bombers sank a German battleship in twenty minutes; the admirals were shocked; he was court martialed.

Hyman Rickover had almost as bad a time trying to sell the nuclear submarine. Submarines have a long history of rejection. In 1897 Simon Lake's *Argonaut* operated successfully in the open sea and was spurned by the U.S. government. Lake wrote in his book *The Submarine in War and Peace* that it took "many years of persistent endeavor and the expenditure of vast sums of money furnished by patriotic individuals, and also . . . recognition . . . by several foreign governments, before our government recognized any merit in my work."

Lake said that "The Wright Brothers' first recognition and the first dollar they ever received as profits in their years of experimental effort came from France." Not from the French military men, you may be sure. When Napoleon was setting out to conquer the world an

 American inventor, Robert Fulton, offered France a submersible, the *Nautilus,* which had made many successful descents. The French Admiralty rejected it, one admiral saying, "Thank God, France still fights her battles on the surface, not beneath it." The English paid Fulton $75,000 for his submarine, and he went on to build the *Clermont* and other steamboats.

"War is much too serious a matter to be entrusted to the military."
—TALLEYRAND, *attributed*

When the United States entered World War I a delegation of representatives of scientific groups went to Washington and formally offered their services to the U.S. Navy. They were politely received, heard, and asked to return the following day for an answer. They did so, and were told, "No thank you. The navy already has a scientist."

After World War I General Billy Mitchell urged the Navy to consider making more use of airplanes. Said Josephus Daniels, Secretary of the Navy, "Good God! This man should be writing dime novels." Said Admiral Charles Benson, Chief of Naval Operations, "I cannot conceive of any use that the fleet will ever have for aircraft . . . aviation is just a lot of noise."

"As far as sinking a ship with a bomb is concerned, you just can't do it."
—REAR-ADMIRAL CLARK WOODWARD, *1939*

Before World War II Charles de Gaulle wrote a manual on tank warfare that was rejected by the French and used by the Germans.

When the Allied invasion of Europe was imminent, Hitler guessed that it would start in Normandy, but his generals disagreed. Then Hitler was fooled by a feint to the north, changed his mind, and rejected the frantic appeals for reinforcement of the Normandy beaches after the invasion had begun. For several days he refused to release troops from the Pas de Calais region. His rejection of his generals' pleas sealed the fate of the southern forces.

Christopher Cooke wrote a thesis on nuclear weapons, twice applied for a job with the CIA, and was twice turned down. He became deputy commander of a Titan II missile-firing crew and volunteered to spy for the Russians.

"Run it up the flagpole"—and if nobody salutes?

Political figures, it seems, are particularly vulnerable to rejection. Nixon was rejected twice before he rejected himself out of the White House.

After he had been defeated for the presidency by Kennedy in 1960 he ran for governor of California and was again defeated. On November 7, 1962, he pronounced himself finished, saying to reporters, "you won't have Nixon to kick around any more. . . ." But he wasn't, and they did. Only his Checkers speech saved him from rejection by Eisenhower as the vice-presidential candidate in 1952. And goodness knows how many other times he was rejected, or fancied himself rejected, by family, friends, enemies, and reporters.

He seems to thrive on rejection, as certain tiny creatures get nourishment out of dead wood, acid, and other unlikely substances.

Maybe he will override rejection once more.

After all, Muhammad Ali (*né* Cassius Clay— he rejected his name for religious reasons) lost the heavyweight boxing title twice and won it back both times.

In 1884 William Tecumseh Sherman rejected the presidency in twelve words: "If nominated I will not run. If elected I will not serve." In 1927 Cal Coolidge used ten: "I do not choose to run for President in 1928." Maybe some day somebody will strip away all of that excess verbiage with a simple "No."

Many people have run for president and been defeated two times. William Jennings Bryan was the first nominated candidate to run and be defeated three times (Democrat, 1896, 1900, 1908). Norman Thomas set a record that may never be surpassed by running unsuccessfully six times as the Socialist Party candidate (1928, 1932, 1936, 1940, 1944, 1948).

Bryan

Thomas with Truman—
Allyn Baum/
The New York Times

"If you can't stand the heat, get out of the kitchen." —HARRY TRUMAN

The case of Harold Stassen was (is) different. In 1944, while he was still in the Navy, he announced that he was "available" for the presidency, but his services were not required. In 1952, 1964, 1968, 1976 and 1980 he ran, unsuccessfully, for the Republican nomination; in 1972 he backed Nixon.

The two most savagely rejected presidents of this century were Herbert Hoover and Jimmy Carter. Hoover was repudiated for Roosevelt in 1932 because of something neither he nor anybody else could control, the Depression; Carter was thrashed by Reagan in 1980 because of something either he or his associates should have been able to mend—his way of doing, and not doing, business. (And in that 1980 election only 52 percent of the eligible voters voted— are we as a nation rejecting our political system?)

"I had not the advantage of a classical education, and no man should . . . accept a degree that he cannot read."
—PRESIDENT MILLARD FILLMORE, *rejecting an honorary degree (written in Latin) from Oxford*

After the Revolution and before our democracy set in, Washington was thrice urged to let himself be crowned king, and thrice refused. Some people think we'd be better off now if he hadn't.

George Washington also refused to accept his $500 monthly salary as a general and instead opted for an expense account. That way, (from 1775 to 1783) he made almost $400,000 more. When he became president he again wanted to take expenses, not a salary of $25,000 per annum. Congress rejected his proposal.

George Washington taking leave of his mother en route to his inauguration.

Our first First Gentleman kept his image untarnished during his life, of course, but afterwards that image—as seen in the most famous portrait ever painted of him—suffered sad and messy rejection.

In 1796 artist Gilbert Stuart painted portraits of George and Martha Washington. George died three years later, and Stuart died in 1828. Mrs. Stuart was destitute and tried to sell the pictures, but both Massachusetts and the federal government refused to buy them. Then, in 1831, the Boston Athenaeum, a private but public-spirited library and art gallery, took pity on the widow and raised $1500 for the two portraits, not because they were very good—they weren't and aren't—but from historic concern and compassion.

In 1867 the Athenaeum helped found Boston's Museum of Fine Arts and lent it the two Stuarts, as well as other art works. The Museum thought little of the portraits and hung them in an obscure place.

A century later the tables were turned. Destitute Mrs. Stuart's benefactor felt the pinch of inflation and needed money. By then the Washingtons were world-renowned, and the Athenaeum offered to sell them to the Museum for $1,633,334, much less than the market price. The Museum said that the pictures were of "historic but not aesthetic interest" and refused to buy them.

In 1977 the Athenaeum renewed its offer and again the Museum rejected it.

In the meantime tentative offers, some of them for more than $7,000,000, poured in from collectors and museums all over the country.

But the Athenaeum felt that the Washingtons' pictures belonged in their own city, and so agreed to accept $5,000,000 (raised by public subscription) from the National Portrait Gallery, with the proviso that for fifty years the Washingtons would spend one year out of every five in Boston.

That mutually beneficial arrangement was almost consummated when the Museum woke from its long apathy, realized what it was losing, and tried—greedily and unbecomingly, dispassionate observers thought—to queer the deal and force the Athenaeum to sell to it for a pittance—two million dollars at most—of what the Portrait Gallery was offering. There ensued an unseemly, most un-Bostonian, brouhaha. The Museum loudly and chauvinistically stirred up misplaced urban patriotism: The Athenaeum was too shocked to respond; for a year or more the land of the Lowells and cods was rent with what George and Martha and their friends would have surely considered an unbelievable display of irresponsible folly.

Not until 1979 did the Museum simmer down, the deal go through, and those poor rejected, rerejected, bewildered ghosts go home.

Since Hoover it has been the custom of every president upon leaving office to have his papers and memorabilia stored in a presidential library, actually a combined archive and museum, owned and operated by the National Archives, and soon after his inauguration Jack Kennedy began thinking about his. In October 1963—a month before Dallas—he arranged for a site located on the grounds of the Harvard Business School in Cambridge, Massachusetts. After his death a great deal of money was raised, and the project was expanded to include a school of government and an institute of politics, to be a part of Harvard. In 1965 the Commonwealth of Massachusetts voted seven million dollars to buy a different site, which JFK had preferred but been unable to get, the twelve acre subway car repair yard of the Metropolitan Transit Authority located between Boylston Street and Memorial Drive along the Charles River in Cambridge.

There was general enthusiasm.

But then came a long delay while the MTA looked for a new home, and opposition to the Kennedy project began to surface: some Cambridge residents feared that the museum would attract so many sightseers that the already saturated Harvard Square area would be overwhelmed.

In 1973 architect I.M. Pei submitted a design for the library complex that featured a giant flat-topped glass pyramid eighty-five feet high. Critics savaged it—"instant Giza," "banal symbolism," "a cross between Camelot and Disneyland." The next year Pei submitted a second, more modest, design, but that too was attacked, with threats of environmental impact lawsuits that could keep the library plans buried in the courts for years. The exasperated Kennedys talked about moving the library out of Cambridge, and immediately more than a hundred cities and towns across the country, from Abilene to Newport, offered themselves as sites.

The embattled Cambridge anti-museumites proposed that the museum be separated from the rest of the complex and go somewhere else, but the Kennedys refused to split the museum from the archive. There were other proposals and counterproposals, charges and denials, refusals. Statistics, two-edged as always, were brandished, and tempers flared. There was unseemly strife in the groves of academe.

At last, late in 1975, a decision was reached. The Kennedys would build the museum and archive on Columbia Point, a spectacular site on the South Boston waterfront, and Harvard would keep the educational institutions in Cambridge.

Two years later—a long fourteen years after the president's death—construction began.

Kennedys are tough. So are Cantabrigians. Both sides won, maybe, and lost, certainly, by the heated two-way rejection.

Nations, supposedly so rapacious for foreign territory (or property), have often been strangely shy when juicy bits were dangled in front of them. During the first half of the last century California was ruled by a weak Mexico which was in turn ruled by a weak Spain; to the north, in Russian Alaska, a shrewd man named Baranov saw the possibility of Muscovite expansion down the coast. For years he tried to persuade his countrymen to seize California and turn the Pacific into a "Russian lake." Saint Petersburg not only rejected his idea of expansion, but by mid-century was trying to contract—by getting rid of Alaska. The United States then had its chance to expand, and proved similarly reluctant. The story of how hard Russia had to work to sell us Alaska is well

known—not so well known, perhaps, is the story, apparently authentic, that the Russian ambassador actually had to bribe a good many U.S. Senators before Congress would approve the purchase of "Seward's Folly." (William Seward, Secretary of State, negotiated the 1867 treaty.) The odd $200,000 of the purchase price of $7,200,000 was recompense to the ambassador for the money spent for those bribes.

Belgium refused to buy the Congo in 1884 and King Leopold II had to pay for it out of his own pocket.

Charles V, Holy Roman Emperor from 1519 to 1556, once received a strange, lumpy, plated something from the mysterious new continent we now call South America. It was said to be edible but he refused to eat it, for fear of poison, and that was a pity because he probably would have enjoyed it. It was a pineapple.

"Our business in this world is not to succeed, but to continue to fail in good spirits."

Momentous rejections destined to affect England, America, and all of the wide realms of knowledge were foreshadowed in 1765 when a "natural" son was born to an English peer, Sir Hugh Smithson. The next year Sir Hugh became the first Duke of Northumberland, and any son of his, even an illegitimate one, was a power in the land. James Smithson was rich and respected. But not, he reckoned, respected enough—because of his bar sinister he was not admitted to the highest levels of society. That rejection never ceased to gall him. He did well at Oxford, became a competent amateur chemist and mineralogist (the ore smithsonite is named for him), and was elected to the Royal Society. But he never made it to the top rank as a scientist, and that failure galled him too.

James Smithson

Toward the end of his life came the rejection that had the historic consequences. He had willed his fortune to the Royal Society, but that body refused to publish one of his scientific papers, and that was the last straw. He changed his will and left everything to a nephew, to be passed on, if the nephew should die without issue, to the United States of America "to found at Washington, under the name to [sic] the Smithsonian Institution, an establishment for the increase & diffusion of Knowledge among men." Smithson had never been to America, had no American friends, and only one known connection with the country: his half-brother, Lord Percy, had commanded the British troops at the battle of Lexington. Publicly he said that science should flourish more under a New World republic than under an Old World monarchy; privately he must have felt the spur of lifelong rejections. He died in 1829, his nephew

died childless in 1835, and a new series of rejections and would-be rejections began.

News of the strange bequest reached Washington when Andrew Jackson was presiding
over twenty-four states and an unruly Congress,
and an uproar broke out at once. Some legislators feared that acceptance of the bequest
might set a precedent whereby "every whipper-
snapper vagabond" would suppose that he could
"have his name distinguished in the same way,"
and others demanded that the legacy be refused
outright, on the grounds that it was "beneath
the dignity of the country to accept such gifts
from foreigners." Since the words *increase &
diffusion of Knowledge* could be interpreted in
many ways, they were, and passionately. Should
the new Institution be a library, a museum, an
art gallery, a laboratory, an observatory, a
school—or what? Ingenious proposals were eloquently advanced and eloquently rejected.

Massachusetts's Rufus Choate wanted a library, "durable as liberty . . . a vast treasury of
all the facts which make up the history of man
and of nature. . . ." Ohio's Robert Dale Owen
thought that a rotten idea. To him the libraries
of "luxurious Europe" were "clouds of windy
verbiage . . . petty antiquarian triumphs [that]
dwarf down into utter insignificancy" in the
light of good modern American practicality. He
proposed that the Smithson money be spent
not for "vast and bloated book-gatherings" but
for a natural history collection, a laboratory, a
garden for farm experiments, and a normal
school, for training teachers. Vermont's George
Perkins Marsh disapproved Owen's laboratory
and approved Choate's library.

Adams

Ex-President John Quincy Adams disapproved both Owen's school—he said he would
rather see "the whole money thrown into the
Potomac" than a single dollar of it spent on
such a silly enterprise—and Choate's library,
and everything else except his own pet project.
He thought that the Smithson bequest should
be used for an astronomical observatory, a
hard-working station with "no sinecures—no
monkish stalls for lazy idlers."

And so it went. Proposals, rejections. And the ever-present danger that there would be one rejection too many, and Smithson's last wish would be denied. But the danger was averted. Congress voted to accept the bequest. In 1838 the money, 105 bags of gold sovereigns valued at $508,318.46, arrived in New York. (Two years later Congress invested most of it in state bonds in Arkansas, which promptly defaulted—Congress made good the loss.) In 1846 the institution was legally established. After eleven tumultuous years "the Smithsonian scandal" was ended—almost. There were a few more complaints and attempted rejections. Andrew Johnson accused the Smithsonian of "sucking the blood" of the taxpayers because it was being paid 6 percent interest on its money by the U.S. Treasury and in 1848 he proposed that the Institution be turned into a school for orphans. In 1852 Stephen A. Douglas tried to turn it into a farm bureau and in 1870 bookman William Poole suggested that it should be consigned to oblivion; he lashed out at it for publishing an astronomical paper rather than his scholarly *Index to Periodical Literature*—"a new orbit for the planet Neptune! The old one is probably worn out"—and hinted darkly that "the world ought to know what the 'most useless' institution in creation is doing. . . ."

But the infant Institution survived the attacks, denials, and rejections, grew strong, and became the internationally famous *increaser & diffuser of Knowledge* that we see today. It is interesting to note that the present Smithsonian has within itself every one of the components suggested for it in the beginning, minus maybe

three—library, normal school, and school for orphans—plus several others including a zoo. And it is sad to note that it, the child of a reject and itself almost a reject, is now a rejecter. Long known and cherished as "The Nation's Attic," it is forever being given things—thimbles, helmets, butter dishes, raccoons—thousands and thousands of things. And most of those things it cannot, alas, accept.

The familiar "willow" pattern on this cup is a scene of mythical rejection. The couple on the bridge are being driven into exile by her father, the Duke.

One of the best and bravest of all rejections took place in 1970 when the U.S. Senate voted against the supersonic transport plane. Lobbying for that plane were powerful arm-twisting groups: Boeing and the rest of the aircraft industry, labor, the Department of Transportation, the French and British governments (which wanted the SST to pave the way for their Concorde), the Nixon White House. Against it were only concerned citizens and a few conservation groups—and the implications of the information they had gathered and disseminated: the SST would generate a sonic boom unsettling to humans and animals and destructive to property; it might destroy the ozone in the upper atmosphere, which protects us from the radiation that can cause, among other undesirable things, skin cancer; it would be brutally expensive to build and wasteful to operate, requiring about one ton of fuel to fly one passenger from New York to London. Influenced only by that information and a rising groundswell of opposition, the Senate shot the plane down. (The next year the whole Congress buried it.) That vote against much-vaunted "progress," by a strong country that could have afforded it but for the best of reasons didn't want it, was unique in history.

Around the globe it was the landing place, rather than the landing machine, that has caused such strife.

Narita airport, forty miles east of Tokyo, has been under attack ever since work on it began in 1967. Farmers whose land was confiscated, radicals, liberals (remember Agnew's righteous rejections of "radlibs" before he was himself rejected?), environmentalists, and students have done their best to put it out of business. According to *Time* (June 5, 1978), "There have been fifty-six major riots and demonstrations, five deaths, 8,100 injuries and 1,900 arrests." One wonders whether any U.S. airport, even a tough Texas one, could survive such rejection.

Allyn Baum/The New York
Times UPI

A Tale of Two Hate-Full Cities

In Texas of the ghost towns there is a ghost airport—created, and killed, by hate.

Dallas and Fort Worth, thirty miles apart, have always despised each other. Fort Worthian Amon Carter hated Dallas so much that (although he was oil-rich enough to buy a hundred restaurants) he took along a sandwich whenever he had to go there so that he wouldn't have to eat Dallas-touched food. His hobby was aviation—he was a director and part owner of American Airlines—and it curled his horns when in the 1930s a Dallas airport, Love Field, began serving both cities.

In 1943 Fort Worth opened Midway Field, so named because it was strategically located half-way between the two cities. During the rest of World War II Midway was used for flight training, but when that war ended Fort Worth and Amon Carter declared their own war on Dallas. They poured millions of dollars into Midway, renamed it Greater Fort Worth International Airport, and went after the Dallas traffic. They tried their best (and a very good best it was—Big Amon owned newspapers and a radio station) to have their field declared the regional airport.

In vain. Dallas enlarged Love.

Fort Worth and Amon Carter spent more money on their field, renamed it Amon Carter Field, and beat the aerial bushes for customers.

Dallas enlarged Love.

Fort Worth Star Telegram

In 1955, when Amon Carter died, the hated enemy was still in the catbird seat, but Fort Worth carried on the feud. More money, more beautification, another name change—in 1960 Amon Carter Field became Greater Southwest International Airport.

Greater, Dallasians asked, than what? Love was by far the busiest airport in the southwest. It was also the hungriest. Between 1959 and 1965 it doubled its passenger traffic, while the number of passengers flying from its rival fell from a skimpy 174,240 per year to an almost invisible 29,131—not even one plane load a day.

Greater Southwest International, as grand and lavish an airport as money could buy, was about as popular as a two-storey outhouse.

Fort Worth, desperate, made many compromise offers. Dallas rejected them all.

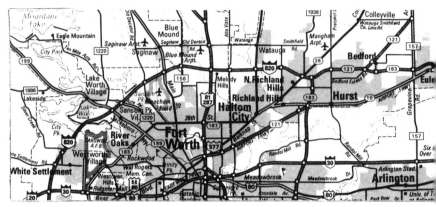

In the late 1960s the long strangulation ended. Midway/GFWI/ACF/GSWI died as a commercial airport and shriveled into a training field for American Airlines.

But the drama of rejection was not played out.

After Love had conquered all it was itself conquered, by geography. In the early 1970s the Civil Aeronautics Board came looking for a site for a regional airport, and rejected busy Love as being too close to a city for future expansion. Somnolent GSWI was rejected for the same reason. In 1974 yet another airport was put into operation down there. Today, Dallas–Fort Worth Field, well north of old Midway, serves both cities.

Although Dallas and Fort Worth still don't like each other on the ground, their thirty-one-year war in the air is finally over. Bones whiten in the Texas sun.

Love Field is now used only by Southwest Airlines and private planes. Greater Southwest International lies buried beneath a real estate development. Office buildings, stores, and parking lots cover Amon Carter's darling—the Ghost of Christmas Never.

Long before Dallas and Fort Worth were

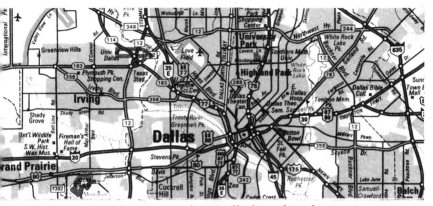

born their home state knew all about hostility and rejection.

The first Europeans to see the region wished, as they died, that they hadn't. In 1527 a raggle-taggle band of Spanish would-be conquistadors, under the hapless Pánfilo de Narváez, suffered so terribly in what is now Florida that they killed and ate their horses, made boats out of the skins, sailed west, and were wrecked on the what is now Texas coast. There they found Nature redder in tooth and claw, and arrow, than it had been in Florida. After six years of battling disease, animals, and Indians, four survivors (not including Pánfilo) reached Mexico.

Other Spaniards came, saw, and were quickly conquered. In 1682 a settlement was attempted on the site of the present El Paso, but it, in the dry words of the history books, "did not flourish." In 1685 La Salle's French adventurers sailed into Matagorda Bay and promptly lost two ships. La Salle was murdered by one of his own men, and the rest of the band were massacred by Indians or disappeared soon after. In 1690 Spaniards founded a mission near the Neches river which was, by contemporary standards, brilliantly successful: it lasted three years.

Not until 1718, almost two centuries after they had first been savaged by it, did Europeans manage to impose a permanent settlement, the Spanish mission at San Antonio, in the unruly southwest territory.

A hundred years later that region, which had so long rejected invaders physically, was rudely rejected itself, politically.

In 1819 the United States signed a treaty with Spain by which we got Florida and renounced all claims to Texas, but in 1821 Mex-

ico won its independence from Spain and right away we tried to buy Texas from the new owner. In 1829 President Jackson offered five million dollars for the province. Mexico haughtily rejected the offer.

In 1832 Stephen F. Austin, "The Father of Texas," presented a petition to the Mexican military dictator, Santa Anna, for separate statehood for Texas. The petition was rejected and so was the petitioner—Austin was thrown into prison and kept there for eighteen months.

In 1835 Texas cut loose from Mexico, and in 1836 formally declared independence and sent two commissioners to Washington. The U.S. government refused to recognize them. In that same year 4000 Mexicans killed 187 Texans at the Alamo, Sam Houston's army won the battle of San Jacinto, and the Republic of Texas officially requested admission to the United States. Because the new republic was pro-slavery our Northern states objected, and President Van Buren said no. In the House of Representatives ex-President John Quincy Adams presented 350 petitions against annexation, and then buried the proposal under a three-week speech (not called a filibuster because at that time the word hadn't been applied to that tac-

REWARD
$200
DEAD OR ALIVE

tic). Texas built a navy, generated a national debt, was recognized by France and England, and in 1837 withdrew the annexation request.

It was cold out there, though, and four years later the Republic renewed the request. And at last, after a lot of national and international intriguing by Republic President Sam Houston, as slick a horse trader as he was a Mexican shooter, the request was granted: in December 1845 Texas became the twenty-eighth state of the Union—and a bone of even fiercer contention.

In what was to prove one of the costliest rejections in history, Mexico refused to accept the annexation of her former property, and went to war with the annexer. She was soundly beaten, and lost all of her remaining property above the Rio Grande, the vast area that is now California, Arizona, Nevada, Utah, parts of New Mexico, Colorado, and Wyoming.

You might have thought that Texas was home free, rejection-proof, after she got her statehood, but no. In 1860 she figured that she needed more land (390,143 square miles being hardly enough to turn around in), and so she simply announced that part of her northern border was the north fork of the Red River, not the south fork as before supposed. She christened her new territory Greer County and settled people and cattle there. Too bad. In 1895 the Supreme Court ruled that the boundary was indeed the south fork of the Red River—the south *bank* of the south fork, to be exact. Greer County became one with Nineveh and Tyre (or worse, from a Texas point of view, Oklahoma).

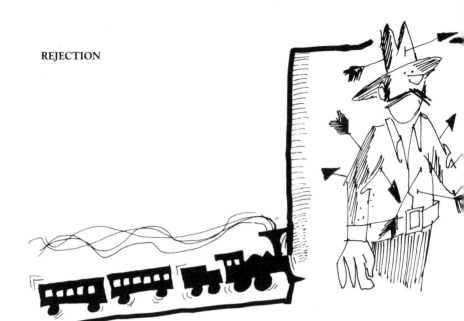

In 1861 three more rejections came in quick succession. In February Texas seceded from the Union. Sam Houston was governor then, and he refused to join the Confederacy. In March the state legislators fired him. The legality of that firing was questioned, and there came offers from the North to help him fight it. He rejected all of the offers and retired.

On January 3, 1959, poor Texas suffered something worse than any rejection—a blow to her pride. Alaska, all 586,412 square miles of

it, became the forty-ninth state. A million jokes and boasts perished on that dreadful day, and the word *largest* had to be yanked out of the Texas state song (which happens to be the largest flop of a state song ever written—when it was first scheduled to be played, in 1924, the band refused to play it).

Never mind. Some day our most rejected state may turn the tables, for Texas cherishes a strange fruit. She came into the Union with an extraordinary unique right—the legal right to split herself into five smaller states any time she wanted to. That right is still there, in the constitution. It periodically excites inflammable Texans, who have, over the years, more or less seriously proposed nearly twenty times that the state split into five parts, to be given such names as San Jacinto, Franklin, Lincoln, Jefferson, and Matagorda.

The prospect of five Lone Star states, with ten U.S. senators, distresses certain Washington legislators, and recently their distress was made more acute.

Houston

In 1975 Texas State Senator Bob Gammage declared that *if* Texas should decide to split into five little Texases, and *if* the U.S. Senate, fearful of those ten Lone Star senators, should oppose that decision, then by cracky there just might occur the rejection to end all rejections— Texas might, in the immortal word of John L. Lewis, disaffiliate—leave the Union—become, once again and for always, a free and independent Republic—sitting on *all that oil*!!!

★ ★ ★ ★

Big ideas get rejected in Texas. In 1855 Congress paid $30,000 to send thirty-four camels to San Antonio to be pack animals for the army. The men wouldn't speak to the ugly things, and neither would the horses. The Civil War came along and ended the embarrassment—the camels went quietly over the hill. In 1965, after the Surgeon General rejected tobacco as bad for your health, a group of Texas businessmen put all of their muscle and money behind Bravo cigarettes, made of pure lettuce. Bravos made it no bigger than Billy Beer, Jimmy Carter's brother Billy's baby.

"How often the deepest convictions of one generation are the rejects of the next."
—LEARNED HAND, *judge*

131

If they grow rejections big in Texas, they grow them with style in Hollywood and the environs of show biz. A Fox reader rejected *Jaws* with the comment that it might make a movie of the week for TV. Universal took it, and of course turned it into one of the top money-making movies of all times. The next year Universal rejected *Star Wars,* and Fox took it.

Producer Richard Barr was on Long Island when a friend asked him to come over to Connecticut and catch a musical show about a simple-minded medieval Spaniard, maybe worthy of Broadway. Barr didn't go. The friend, Al Selden, found another partner, Hal James, and overnight Broadway went back into the Middle Ages with *Man of La Mancha.*

The next time Selden called about a promising play, *Drat*, Barr hurried over to see it, and with his partner Charles Woodward took it to Broadway. It closed after one night.

The play *Never Too Late*, about a middle-aged couple surprised by the stork, bounced around the weeds for six years, getting rejected by two dozen producers before Elliot Martin decided to take a chance on it. Martha Scott turned down the female lead, and Maureen O'Sullivan accepted it only because she figured that she would be back home with her husband and seven children in a week or less. That play ran for three years.

Life With Father, a comedy about a cranky man, had similar un-appeal in the egg. So many experts turned the script down that would-be producer Oscar Serlin, desperately looking for an angel, sneaked it into a suitcase belonging to occasional angel John Hay Whitney. Whitney's theatrical adviser was Robert Benchley, and he thought the play stank: "I could smell it as the postman came whistling down the lane. Don't put a dime in it." Whitney disagreed. Walter Huston rejected the title

---

"Usually I find out I'm unemployed by reading the papers." —TIM CONWAY, *actor*

---

role, twice, and Alfred Lunt and Lynn Fontanne also declined. Fontanne said she didn't want to spend every night on the stage getting her husband baptized (one of the funniest scenes of the play). At last Howard Lindsay, who had coauthored the script and had not acted for five years, took the part and his wife acted opposite. The play opened in 1939 and ran for seven and a half years.

Producer Robert Whitehead (A Man For All Seasons, The Prime of Miss Jean Brodie) thought that Shaw's Pygmalion "wouldn't be made any richer with music." Producer Cheryl Crawford thought otherwise. At first Alan Jay Lerner and Frederick Loewe refused to write the music, but at last they did, and turned the modestly successful play into the super-musical My Fair Lady.

Crawford had her share of strike-outs, of course. She had a chance to do West Side Story but turned it down because it was, oh you know, too thin, not funny enough. . . .

After one of his plays had closed almost before it opened Bertolt Brecht said, "Ah well, a man is measured by the size and number of his flops."

In the ferociously competitive crowded-as-a-coral-reef jungle of entertainment there are so many suitors for the hand of fickle Princess Fortune that all of them must suffer rejection often, some of them all of the time. (Lucky for them there is no penalty for rejection except poverty—in nursery tales the suitors who fail to please the princess are put to death.)

"We don't like their sound. Groups of guitars are on the way out." —Decca Recording Co., *turning down the Beatles, 1962*

Capitol Records, Inc.

UPI

The Beatles were rejected innumerable times before Parlophone took them on in 1962.

The rock group now called Boston also struck out repeatedly with the main "labels," the recording companies that produce practically all popular music today, until a couple of freelancers, Charley McKenzie and rap Paul Ahern, liked their sound and sold them to Epic Records, which had rejected them before. The first Boston album, released in August 1976, made "the biggest debut in the history of recorded music," *Rolling Stone* magazine reported, "Gold [a million dollars' worth of records] in seven weeks, platinum [a million records] in eleven weeks, twice that in sixteen. . . ." More than seven million of the albums have now been sold in this country alone.

A Grammy Award went to Joe Brooks, who wrote the words and music for the phenomenally successful song "You Light Up My Life." At the presentation ceremony he said, in a neutral tone, "As I look out there tonight, I can't help but think that just about every company out there turned this song down. As a matter of fact, I think that about ten of you turned it down twice, so I must admit this tastes so sweet."

The Muppet Show, perhaps the best loved contemporary television program in the world, was initially rejected steadfastly for nearly two decades by every network it was offered to. The first Muppets, created and operated by Jim Henson and his wife, began appearing on local TV in Washington some twenty years ago, and achieved considerable success. Steve Allen had

them as guests on the old *Tonight Show*, they became regulars on *The Ed Sullivan Show*, and Rowlf the Dog was a fixture on *The Jimmy Dean Show*. In 1970 they took up permanent residence on *Sesame Street* and for a while they were on *Saturday Night Live*. They did specials, two of which won Emmys.

And all the while the networks just stood there. Even though that show, a proven crowd-pleaser and potential block-buster, was running around like a charming waif crying to be adopted, they refused to pick it up.

Henson all but abandoned hope of ever getting network sponsorship. Then help came from afar. Sir Lew Grade, an aggressive English impresario, took the Muppets under his syndicated wing—and sold them back to their native land! Now the show is taped in London and aired across the British Isles and some 100 other countries, in almost as many languages, and is seen here on more than 156 stations. It is enormously popular. Kermit the Frog, Gonzo, Fozzie Bear, Miss Piggy, and Rowlf and friends had to look a long time but they finally found a sugar daddy—that is, a daddy who recognized sugar when he saw it.

Rejection, the brusquer the better, was of course the name of the game and the heart of the fun in that sturdy old TV standby *The Gong Show*.

"Two of the cruelest, most primitive punishments our town deals out . . . are the empty mailbox and the silent telephone."
—HEDDA HOPPER

Harvard Theatre Collection

When Fred Astaire first offered himself to Hollywood he was rejected as being only "a balding, skinny actor who can dance a little."

There isn't always a close correlation between an aspiring actor's screen test and ultimate performance.

Bette Davis's first test was so bad that she ran screaming out of the room. Gable failed his first two tests because he seemed to Jack Warner to be only a big ape, and then because his ears were too big. Brigitte Bardot failed a screen test at age sixteen because she had puppy fat and spots.

Julie Andrews scored a huge success in *My Fair Lady* on Broadway but was rejected by Hollywood for the movie. That she was as good on film as on the stage, if not better, was amply demonstrated later by her movie performances in *The Sound of Music* and *Mary Poppins*.

139

Charlie's Angels jiggled past some very unmannerly rejections from without and—Heaven help us!—from within.

In 1974 producer Leonard Goldberg proposed a TV series featuring female detectives. Everybody agreed that the idea was hopeless. ABC expressed it most succinctly: "crazy." Goldberg and partner Aaron Spelling tried to get Ernest (*The French Connection*) Tidyman to script it. He wrote one draft and quit. Actor Robert Wagner was offered a 45 percent interest and said "worst idea I've ever heard." And so it went. And so, naturally, it finally triumphed, came to the tube in 1976 and landed right on the top of the ratings.

Feminists hated it. Andrea Dworkin, author of *Pornography: Men Possessing Women,* was "totally disgusted. . . ." Kate Jackson (Angel Sabrina) said, "This show is so light that it would take a week to get to the ground if you dropped it from the ceiling," and got herself fired. Farrah Fawcett (Angel Jill) quit, and so did various replacements.

But the Angels jiggled on through 109 revealing episodes before they folded their wings in June, 1981.

But let not T&A aficionados despair. Dead Angels don't go to Heaven. They go into syndication, and rerun, or rejiggle, forever and ever Amen.

Others may agree with the epitaph pronounced on the show by the only man in it, actor David Doyle (Bosley): "There won't be another one like it—which opens the way for a lot of people to say, 'Thank God.' "

Said Goldberg, "Our next show is about garbage collectors."

Here's your hat; what's your hurry?

A Spelling-Goldberg Production

In 1970 George C. Scott was awarded an Oscar for his acting in *Patton*, and refused to accept the prize. In 1972 so did Marlon Brando, for *The Godfather*.

The author Willa Cather left instructions in her will that none of her books may ever be made into a movie.

Jean–Léon Gérôme, *Pollice Verso* ("Thumbs Down"), Phoenix Art Museum Collection

Barbara Eden was offered $100,000 (all commercials seem to go for either 100 or 25 thou) to hustle Thomas's English Muffins. She refused, because she didn't want to look like the girl next door. (She wound up looking like a houri from Arabia in "I Dream of Jeannie").

Raquel Welch rejected an offer of $200,000 to do a thirty-second spot for one dog food company and John Wayne turned down a quarter of a million to do the like for another.

It wasn't that they didn't like dogs. They just didn't think they could come out smelling as sweet as that lovable old hound-hugger Lorne Greene.

Sir Laurence Olivier did consent to snap a picture for a Polaroid commercial for $275,000—but he stipulated that the demeaning performance should not be shown in his native England.

Howard Cosell's agent said $100,000 or no deal to Canada Dry's offer to put him on the "Not Too Sweet" plug but there was a deal—The Mouth talked for $25,000. Tennis player Jimmy Connors, of whom Cosell has said many mean things, did the same commercial for $50,000.

Xerox wanted the great French mime Marcel Marceau to do a commercial. Marceau's agent said *oui*, for $100,000. Xerox said *non*. Celebrity-stroker Lloyd Kolmer got to work. He talked and talked to the king of silence and finally made an offer he couldn't refuse—$25,000. Marcel said *oui*, and for the commercial won a Clio, the ad business's Oscar.

French chef Julia Child has no *appetit, bon* or otherwise, for commercials. She will not do them at all.

Neither will Walter Cronkite. Nor, for that matter, Ronald Reagan (anymore), the Ayatollah Khomeini, Jimmy Carter, or the Reverend Moon.

Rejection can be, like cleanliness, next to Godliness.

A TV commercial was rejected after a single showing because it was too suggestive. One night a Xerox spot showed a chimpanzee operating a copying machine, to demonstrate how easy it was. The next morning a thousand secretaries found two thousand bananas on their desks. *The End.*

Most actors and actresses reject their real names for others of supposedly greater appeal. Some examples:

Dirk Bogarde (Derek Julius Gaspard Ulric Niven van den Bogaerde)

Laurence Harvey (Larushka Mischa Skikne)

Walter Matthau (Walter Matasschanskayasky)

Sandra Dee (Alexandra Zuck)

Doris Day (Doris Kappelhoff)

Dean Martin (Dino Crocetti)

Robert Taylor (Spangler Arlington Brugh)

An extraordinary drama of wholesale and retail rejection was played out in the late 1930s. *Gone with the Wind* was being filmed and the most passionately watched search of the century was on—the search for the actress who would play that sweet-and-sour Georgia peach Scarlett O'Hara. A crinoline-frilled army of sixty (some say six hundred) beautiful and otherwise American girls, plenty of them as Southern as mint julep, tried for the part. After three years of wall-to-wall rejection and mounting tension, bust mah buttons, Aunt Pitty Pat!, an English girl got the part! Vivien Leigh???

Pandemonium! Worse than a damn yankee!

The South riz again. Miss Leigh (who hadn't wanted the part all that much anyway) had to be protected by armed guards when she came to Atlanta for the film's world premiere on December 15, 1939. On her way into the theater she was booed louder than any of the Salem witches walking to the gallows. On her way out she was cheered. Even the United Daughters of the Confederacy buried the bloody flag. Said they: "She is Scarlett to the life . . . and has immortalized the best of our distaff forebears."

It now seems impossible that any of the other three finalists for the role—Joan Bennett, Jean Arthur, Paulette Goddard—could have played Scarlett as well as the English girl did.

"Frankly, my dear . . ."

From the MGM release "Gone With the Wind" © 1939 Selznick International Pictures, Inc. Copyright renewed 1967 by Metro-Goldwyn-Mayer Inc.

Apparently the first movie review, of *May Irwin Kiss* in 1896, was a rejection: " . . . absolutely disgusting."

The Guinness Book of World Records says that the shortest dramatic criticism ever delivered was Wolcott Gibbs's characterization of the play *Wham!*—the single word "Ouch!" But *The Book of Failures* disagrees. It says that the play *A Good Time* got the review "No."

According to *Guinness*, many plays have opened and closed on the same night, the most expensive being *Kelly* ($700,000, February 6, 1965), but the rapid-reject record goes to *The Intimate Revue*, which closed (March 11, 1930) after less than one complete performance—seven scenes were cut.

"I played over the music of that scoundrel Brahms. What a giftless bastard!"
—PETER ILICH TCHAIKOVSKY, 1886

Brahms   Tchaikovsky

Culture (whether high or low) has a long history of rejection. It is said that violinists tried to reject some of the scores Beethoven wrote because, they claimed, they were so difficult that they simply could not be played. But the composer insisted that they could be, and he was right.

Of course, strikes are rejections carried to the end of the line, sometimes with tragic, sometimes with ludicrous results.

Many fine newspapers have died because striking unions have not been able to reconcile differences.

"If Beethoven's Seventh Symphony is not by some means abridged, it will soon fall into disuse."
—Philip Hale, *Boston music critic, 1837*

During Act III of a recent West German performance of Wagner's *Die Meistersinger* the audience was first puzzled, then astonished, then amused or disgusted, according to individual tastes, when no sound came from the stage—the singers, on strike, were simply mouthing their parts.

WAGNER COMPOSING.

Fidelio, Beethoven's only opera, was first produced in Vienna in 1805 and suffered mild rejection twice, because of war and because it wasn't very good. And both times the ghost of Mozart made things worse. Its troubles began during rehearsals. As Emil Ludwig tells the story in his biography, *Beethoven: Life of a Conqueror,* "The singers were unhappy. . . . The young woman who sang Fidelio gave away her secret . . . because of an enormous bosom," and the man who sang Pizarro, a Herr Mayer, "called out at a difficult point . . . 'My brother-in-law would never have written such damned nonsense!' Everyone knew that his brother-in-law was Mozart." Napoleon's soldiers were approaching, and "a week before the premiere they entered the city. . . . Who would go to the theater. . . ? It was half empty on three successive nights."

Despite that "honorable burial" Beethoven did not abandon hope. He revised and shortened the opera, and it was staged again four months later. "Two performances enjoyed a superficial success," but the reviews were unfavorable, and there was a typically Beethovenesque row. The ever-irascible composer accused the theater manager of not paying him his proper share of the receipts; the manager pointed out that the gallery had not been filled; Beethoven shouted, "I don't compose for the masses," and the manager said, "Even Mozart was not ashamed to write for the gallery." That did it. "The unfortunate words *even Mozart* were too much," says Ludwig. Deeply insulted, Beethoven cried: "Give me back my score!", and *Fidelio* was buried again.

Red-headed Hector Berlioz was a fighter who had a lot to fight. As a student at the Paris Conservatory he was cordially detested by the director, Luigi Cherubini, who once chased him around a table and for three years black-balled him for the Prix de Rome; Berlioz won that prize only after Liszt had praised his *Fantastic Symphony*, which he wrote after he had been rejected by a girl. His *Romeo and Juliet, Benvenuto Cellini,* and *Damnation of Faust* were coolly received in Paris, although applauded elsewhere, and six years before his death in 1869 his last opera, *Les Troyens,* was hissed off the stage.

Caricature du « Journal amusant » (28 novembre 1863)

Liszt

Palestrina

The same Cherubini who chased Berlioz around the table and stood between him and the Prix de Rome refused to permit César Franck to compete for that prize because he was Belgian and refused to admit Franz Liszt into the conservatory because he was Hungarian. In 1933 Arnold Schoenberg was dismissed from the Prussian Academy of Arts because he was a Jew. Pope Paul IV dismissed Giovanno Pierluigi da Palestrina from the college of singers of the papal chapel because he was married (according to Helen Kaufmann the dismissal plunged Palestrina into "the sixteenth century equivalent of a nervous breakdown.") The Duke of Wurttemberg fired his secretary, Carl Maria von Weber, because some money was missing (although the young composer was declared innocent of theft). Franz Schubert was "encouraged to withdraw" from teaching in his father's village school because "musical notations took the place of corrections in his pupils' exercise books." In 1848 Richard Wagner was banished from Dresden because of revolutionary activities and in 1905 Nikolai Rimsky-Korsakov was dismissed from the St. Petersburg Conservatory for the same reason (different revolution). Gustav Mahler was fired as director of the Imperial Opera in Vienna because of the jealousy of other musicians, and Edward MacDowell was invited to become the head of the newly created Department of Music at Columbia University in 1894 and forced to resign after only eight years because he was "a babe in the Columbia woods"—faculty intrigues were too much for him.

Von Weber

Berlioz
in life

and death

Ravel was rejected for the Prix de Rome so often and so unjustly that at last public sentiment forced the man responsible for the rejections, Director Dubois of the Paris Conservatory, to resign.

When Mozart was concertmaster for the orchestra of Archbishop Hieronymus of Salzburg he asked permission to go on a concert tour and was refused and, it is said, was rejected *per pedem*—by foot: the archbishop's steward kicked him out of the room. He then rejected his rejecter and the place of his rejection: he left Salzburg and never came back.

Frank Gersdana

Charles Ives, now considered one of this country's foremost composers, spent most of his working life being rejected by three groups of people: the public, the critics, and other musicians. Especially other musicians. In 1914 a famous German violinist, Franz Milcke, visited Ives and, in the composer's words, "after a lot of big talk, started to play the first movement of the First Sonata. He didn't even get through the first page. He was all bothered with the rhythms and the notes, and got mad. He said

'This cannot be played. It is awful. It is not music, it makes no sense. . . . When you get awfully indigestible food in your stomach . . . you can get rid of it, but I cannot get those horrible sounds out of my ears. . . ." Such comments distressed Ives so much that he decided that "if I wanted to write music that, to me, seemed worth while, I must keep away from musicians. . . ." He did, and he did.

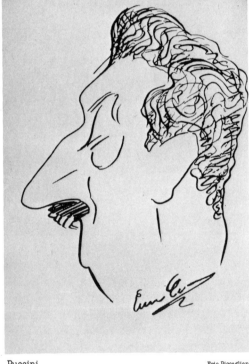

Puccini   Erio Piccagliani

Puccini's *Madama Butterfly*, now one of the most popular of all operas, was a dismal flop on its opening night in Milan in 1904.

Verdi was putting the finishing touches to *Il Trovatore* when a friend dropped in. The friend was a critic whose opinion the composer valued, so he showed him the score, and played the "Anvil Chorus" on the piano. Then he asked the friend what he thought of it. The connoisseur said, "Trash." Verdi chuckled, and played some more, and again asked for an opinion. The friend said, "Rubbish."

Verdi got up and hugged him. The friend asked him why he had done that, and Verdi said, "I have been composing a popular opera. In it I determined to please everybody except the great judges and classicists like you. Had I pleased you, I should have pleased no one else; but your disdain assures me of success. In three months *Il Trovatore* will be sung, roared, whistled, and barrel-organed all over Italy."

Mozart's opera *The Escape from the Seraglio* charmed Vienna when it was first produced but the composer's patron, the emperor Joseph II, spurned it, remarking that it "had too many notes."

Don Hunstein/CBS

Musical rejections can be so vociferous as to drown out the music. When Stravinsky's *avant-avant-garde* ballet, *The Rite of Spring,* was first performed in Paris in 1913 there was a riot. Despite the fact that the great Pierre Monteux was conducting and the even greater Nijinsky was dancing, the audience, shocked by the dissonant and barbarous-sounding music, could not restrain itself. As the composer himself later reported:

> *. . . the first bars of the prelude . . . at once evoked derisive laughter. . . . These demonstrations, at first isolated, soon became general, provoking counter-demonstrations and very quickly developing into a terrific uproar. . . . Diaghileff kept ordering the electricians to turn the lights on or off, hoping in that way to put a stop to the noise. . . .*

Sans succès. Needless to say, the ballet survived that initial rejection. Indeed, its music went on to win the ultimate accolade of a certain kind of popularity—a scant quarter-century after it had turned that Paris audience into howling savages it was charming little children in Disney's *Fantasia.*

The Rite of Spring
Le Sacre du Printemps

First Part
ADORATION OF THE EARTH
Première Partie
L'ADORATION DE LA TERRE

IGOR STRAVINSKY
Revised 1947
New edition 1967

INTRODUCTION

B. & H. 19441

Printed in England

Bizet's *L'Arlesienne* was "coldly received," and the audience was "unresponsive" to the first appearance of his now-famous *Carmen.* He died thinking himself a failure.

"Indifference or derision" greeted most of the works of César Franck when they were first offered.

When Shostakovich's opera *Lady Macbeth of Mzensk* was first performed it was excoriated for its "unbuttoned" scenes, and Stalin walked out.

Arnold Schoenberg's works were first greeted with "hisses and jeers" and other, stronger marks of disapproval. Very well. In 1920 he founded, in Berlin, "The Society for Private Musical Performances." The public be damned.

"Taken as a whole, the universe is absurd." —WALTER SAVAGE LANDOR

Index

Index

Index

Index

Index

Index